Get in Shape, Stay in Shape

 P9-DUM-214

Get in Shape, Stay in Shape

*F. Skip Latella, Winifred Conkling, and
the Editors of Consumer Reports Books*

GET IN SHAPE, STAY IN SHAPE

CONSUMERS UNION

Mount Vernon · New York

GV
481
G46
1989

L C

Special thanks to Donald Mays for his assistance in reviewing the contents of this book, to Robin Raposa for her generosity and patience in modeling for the exercise photographs, and to David May and Steve Wegener for additional photography.

Neither the authors nor the publisher assume any responsibility for any injuries or medical or health-related problems resulting from the use of the exercises and physical fitness programs described in this book. Before engaging in any strenuous physical activity or exercise program, you should consult with your physician, particularly if you are aged 35 or older.

Copyright © 1989 by F. Skip Latella and Consumers Union of United States, Inc., Mount Vernon, New York, 10553
All rights reserved, including the right of reproduction in whole or in part in any form.

Library of Congress Cataloging-in-Publication Data
Get in shape, stay in shape.
Includes index.
1. Exercise.   2. Physical fitness.   I. Latella,
F. Skip.   II. Conkling, Winifred.   III. Consumer Reports
Books.
GV481.G46   1988   613.7'1   88-71027
ISBN 0-89043-243-0

Design by Jackie Schuman
Photographs by Ken Tannenbaum, except those in chapter 6
Line drawings by Robert Melendez

First printing, February 1989
Manufactured in the United States of America

Get in Shape, Stay in Shape is a Consumer Reports Book published by Consumers Union, the nonprofit organization that publishes Consumer Reports, the monthly magazine of test reports, product Ratings, and buying guidance. Established in 1936, Consumers Union is chartered under the Not-For-Profit Corporation Law of the State of New York.

The purposes of Consumers Union, as stated in its charter, are to provide consumers with information and counsel on consumer goods and services, to give information on all matters relating to the expenditure of the family income, and to initiate and to cooperate with individual and group efforts seeking to create and maintain decent living standards.

Consumers Union derives its income solely from the sale of Consumer Reports and other publications. In addition, expenses of occasional public service efforts may be met, in part, by nonrestrictive, noncommercial contributions, grants, and fees. Consumers Union accepts no advertising or product samples and is not beholden in any way to any commercial interest. Its Ratings and reports are solely for the use of the readers of its publications. Neither the Ratings nor the reports nor any Consumers Union publications, including this book, may be used in advertising or for any commercial purpose. Consumers Union will take all steps open to it to prevent such uses of its materials, its name, or the name of Consumer Reports.

Table 1. Adapted from Henry J. Montoye, et al., "Heart Rate Response to a Modified Harvard Step Test: Males and Females, Age 10–69," Research Quarterly 40, no. 1.

Table 2. Copyright © 1983 by Metropolitan Life Insurance Company.

Tables 3 and 4. Adapted from M. L. Pollock, et al., Health and Fitness through Physical Activity (New York: John Wiley & Sons, 1978).

Table 5. Adapted from C. R. Myers, The Official YMCA Physical Fitness Handbook (New York: Popular Library, 1977).

Table 8. Adapted from Ivan Kusinitz, Morton Fine, Physical Fitness for Practically Everybody (Mount Vernon, N.Y.: Consumers Union, 1983).

The four-part test for muscular strength (page 5). Adapted from Perry Johnson, et al., Sports, Exercise and You (New York: Holt, Rinehart and Winston, 1975).

6-4-90

CONTENTS

INTRODUCTION

Many exercise and fitness books promise to let you in on the best system for getting in shape. However, most books overlook the first rule for fitness: No single system of training works for everyone.

Get in Shape, Stay in Shape gives you the information you need to design your own fitness program. You may be surprised at how much you can accomplish with little more than the resolve to start and stay with a regular exercise routine. You do not have to spend endless hours at the gym or run 20 miles every week. You do not have to buy expensive athletic equipment or join a health club. To get in shape, you will have to exert yourself with reasonable limits and make a commitment to exercise regularly; sporadic exercise won't bring the rewards of fitness.

Regular exercise is a vital component of overall health. Fitness is not simply a matter of good genes; it requires taking responsibility for your health. A sensible exercise program will help promote overall well-being—not only physical health, but mental and emotional health as well. In addition to conditioning your body, exercise can also help relieve the effects of stress, provide a sense of personal accomplishment, and improve self-esteem. Regular exercise can help you look and feel your best.

Physical fitness also helps you perform at your best. When you're in good shape, you can make it through the day without exhaustion and still have enough energy left over for leisure activities. Exercise helps your body work more efficiently, and it can reduce the risk of some illnesses.

Exercise is not an antidote for detrimental behavior, however. Working out cannot undo the damage of poor eating habits or tobacco addiction, for example. But studies show that people who exercise regularly tend to improve their other health habits as well.

How to Use This Book

Get in Shape, Stay in Shape offers sound, straightforward information, but it cannot substitute for advice from a doctor familiar with your medical history. Before engaging in any strenuous activity or exercise program, you should consult your physician.

In chapter 1, "What Kind of Shape Are You In?," you will learn how to assess your current fitness level by taking a five-point fitness test. You can then use the results of the self-assessment test and the tips outlined in chapter 2, "Goals and Expectations," to set your fitness goals and define your exercise expectations. About half the people who start an exercise program quit within the first six months. If you set realistic goals, you'll be more likely to stick to your exercise routine.

Once you decide what you want to get out of your exercise program, chapter 3, "Fitness Fundamentals," provides information on the guidelines for exercising. This chapter will help you design a program that targets your fitness objectives: improving your cardiovascular fitness, losing weight, building strength. Chapter 4, "Choosing an Exercise Program," offers advice on selecting exercises and activities.

Before you get started, you will need to familiarize yourself with the basic warm-up, cool-down, and strengthening and stretching exercises shown in chapter 5, "Breaking a Sweat." This chapter shows you which stretches you should do before and after your workout, and suggests exercises for strengthening the major muscle groups: upper body, torso, and legs.

Some people prefer exercising in the privacy and convenience of home, while others prefer working out at a gym or health club. Chapter 6, "Exercising at Home," contains many tips about buying and using home exercise equipment. Chapter 7, "Choosing a Health Club," provides consumer guidelines for selecting a health club.

Many exercise injuries can be prevented, and chapter 8, "Common Injuries and Their Prevention," suggests ways of avoiding injury through muscle strengthening and through stretching. Chapter 9, "Exercise and Older Persons," includes a discussion of special exercises and tips on ways exercises can be modified to satisfy the needs of older people.

Get in Shape, Stay in Shape can be used to develop and alter your exercise routine as your needs, your goals, and your body change over time. One caution: Don't overdo it. No exercise routine can change your life or your body overnight. The benefits of exercise can only be achieved gradually. That's not to say you won't start to feel better quickly—you will. If you exercise regularly, in just a few weeks you should begin to lose weight, build muscle strength and endurance, improve flexibility, and improve your cardiovascular fitness level. As you begin to enjoy the benefits of exercise, you'll find it even easier to stay with your exercise program.

Get in Shape, Stay in Shape

1

What Kind of Shape Are You In?

No single definition of physical fitness satisfies everyone. To an Olympic athlete, fitness might mean the ability to break a world record in the 440-yard dash. To a more sedentary person, fitness might mean nothing more than the ability to perform the routine chores of everyday life.

Although performance standards vary, most exercise experts recognize five basic components of physical fitness:

1. **Aerobic fitness or cardiorespiratory endurance.** The ability to do moderately strenuous activity over a period of time. It reflects how well your heart and lungs work to supply your body with oxygen during exercise.

2. **Body composition.** The proportion of fat to bone and muscle.

3. **Muscular strength.** The ability to exert maximum force. Lifting the heaviest weight you can in a single exertion is an example of muscular strength.

4. **Muscular endurance.** The ability to repeat a movement many times, or to hold a particular position for a prolonged period, for example, the work required to lift a weight 20 times or to hold it up for five minutes.

5. **Flexibility.** The ability to move a joint through its full range of motion and elasticity of the muscle.

A well-rounded exercise program should develop each fitness component.

Should You Talk to Your Doctor Before Exercising?

You should consult a doctor before starting an exercise program, particularly if any of the following applies to you:

- you haven't had a medical checkup in more than two years
- you're over 35
- you're more than 20 pounds overweight (see "Body Composition," page 2)
- you have high blood pressure
- you have high cholesterol
- you've ever had a heart attack, rapid heart palpitations, or a pain in your chest during vigorous activity, such as shoveling snow
- you've ever taken digitalis, nitroglycerin, quinidine, or *any* other heart medication
- your doctor has told you that you have angina pectoris, fibrillation or tachycardia, an abnormal electrocardiogram (EKG), a heart murmur, rheumatic heart disease, or *any* other heart trouble
- you smoke cigarettes
- you have a blood relative who has died of a heart attack before age 60
- you have diabetes
- you have asthma, emphysema, or any other lung condition
- you get out of breath easily
- you have arthritis or rheumatism
- you lead a sedentary life-style

When you do visit your doctor, he or she will give you a physical examination, including measurements of height, weight, and blood pressure, as well as a blood test to measure cholesterol levels. Your doctor may suggest you take a cardiac stress test, which usually costs from $250 to $450.

Chances are the doctor won't recommend a stress test unless you're in a high-risk group. Risk factors for coronary disease include: elevated blood cholesterol, smoking, hypertension, a family history of coronary disease, diabetes, and a sedentary life-style. Any male over 35 with one or more coronary risk factors and any female over 40 with *two* or more risk factors is considered to be in a high-risk group. If your doctor recommends you take a stress test, ask him or her to suggest a facility. If your doctor won't make a recommendation, choose a facility that employs a cardiologist to supervise the test, and make sure there's emergency equipment available.

During a stress test, a doctor monitors your blood pressure and the electrical activity of your heart first while you're resting and then while you're either walking or jogging on a treadmill or pedaling a stationary bicycle. The test is designed to detect heart problems and arterial obstructions that don't always show up on resting electrocardiograms.

After evaluating your health, your doctor can provide you with guidelines about if and how to exercise. You may want to bring this book to see if he or she approves any of the programs and exercises in it.

A Five-Point Fitness Test

After you have received a physician's clearance to exercise, you can begin designing your fitness program. Start by taking the following tests to assess your level of fitness.

Aerobic Fitness   Your pulse rate provides an effective measurement of your aerobic condition, the most important component of physical fitness. When you wake up in the morning, your pulse rate is the lowest it will be all day. As you go through your daily activities, your pulse rate fluctuates as your activity levels change. The more strenuous the activity, the more oxygen your mus-

cles need and the harder your cardiorespiratory system has to work.

Generally, the faster your pulse rate for a given intensity and duration of exercise, the less efficient your heart and lungs are at delivering oxygen to your body. The slower your pulse, the higher your level of aerobic fitness.

If occasional vigorous activity leaves you panting and your heart pounding, you already know you need to work on aerobic endurance. The modified step test offers another way to evaluate aerobic fitness. *Caution:* Attempt this test only after you've consulted a doctor.

First, ask a friend with a stopwatch or a watch with a sweep second hand to time you. Then, at the signal to begin, step up on a stair or bench that is eight inches off the ground, then step down again. Continue stepping up and down, alternating feet, for three minutes at a rate of 24 steps per minute (about two steps every five seconds). Stop at exactly three minutes and walk slowly around the room. Exactly one minute after you've completed the test, count your pulse for ten seconds. (See page 13 for instructions on how to take your pulse.) Multiply by six to get your recovery score.

Use table 1 to assess your fitness level. If you earned a low score in aerobic fitness, you should work on improving your cardiovascular endurance. Exercises described in chapter 4 can help.

Body Composition   Body composition refers to your percentage of body fat, not your weight. You can't determine your exact body composition by consulting standard height-and-weight tables, but the tables can give you a rough indication of whether or not you're overweight.

Most height-and-weight charts provide a considerable range of acceptable weights for any given height. For example, the weight charts say a medium-framed woman five feet seven inches tall should weight between 133 and 147 pounds.

The pinch-an-inch test can also help you determine your body composition. Locate a fold of skin and subcutaneous fat, the layer of fat beneath the skin, and grasp it between your thumb and forefinger. The back of the upper arm, the side of the lower chest, the back of the calf, and the abdomen are good places to test. Pinch the fold

TABLE 1 **Modified Step-Test Evaluation**					
Age	Excellent	Very Good	Good	Fair	Poor
FEMALE					
10–19	Below 82	82–90	92–96	98–102	Above 102
20–29	Below 82	82–86	88–92	94– 98	Above 98
30–39	Below 82	82–88	90–94	96– 98	Above 98
40–49	Below 82	82–86	88–96	98–102	Above 102
50–59	Below 86	86–92	94–98	100–104	Above 104
60–69	Below 86	86–92	94–98	100–104	Above 104
MALE					
10–19	Below 72	72–76	78–82	84–88	Above 88
20–29	Below 72	72–78	80–84	86–92	Above 92
30–39	Below 76	76–80	82–86	88–92	Above 92
40–49	Below 78	78–82	84–88	90–94	Above 94
50–59	Below 80	80–84	86–90	92–96	Above 96
60–69	Below 80	80–84	86–90	92–96	Above 96

of skin, then measure its thickness. If you can pinch more than one inch, you're probably too fat. Read chapter 3 for the best ways to reduce your percentage of body fat, but don't attempt any substantial weight loss without consulting a doctor. If you can pinch less than one-half inch, you may be too thin. If you're too thin, you should consult a doctor. A doctor can show you productive ways to gain weight.

There are more precise methods of determining body fat, such as underwater weighing, skinfold caliper measurements, and high-tech techniques using infrared light, sound waves, or electrical currents.

One of the most accurate of those methods is underwater or hydrostatic weighing. In this method, you sit in a chair attached to a huge scale. You are weighed, then submerged and weighed again, underwater. The amount of body fat can be calculated using a formula based on the fact that lean body tissue is denser than fat (muscle sinks, fat floats). Hydrostatic weighing is accurate to within one percent.

Another reliable method of determining body composition is the skinfold caliper test. The skinfold caliper test is similar to the pinch-an-inch test, except that special calipers measure the pinch to provide an estimate of percentage of body fat. The calipers are calibrated on the assumption that

about half the body's fat is stored just beneath the skin. The skinfold caliper test is accurate to within 3 to 5 percent.

One test of body composition that has been promoted heavily is the electrical impedance test. Some companies charge a hefty fee to conduct the test. The electrical impedance test measures electrical resistance in various parts of the body. The test is based on the principle that lean tissue, bone and muscle largely made up of water, has a far greater electrolyte content than fat, and on the assumption that the less electrical resistance measured (the more electrolytes) the more lean tissue and less fat. Water and bone content, however, vary tremendously from person to person and affect body density independently of fat. Also, sweating, drinking, eating, and exercise change a person's water content from day to day. Therefore the electrical impedance test can be inaccurate and yield unreliable results.

Although hydrostatic weighing and the skinfold caliper test yield more accurate estimates of the percentage of body fat than do height-and-weight tables, they can be costly. There's really no need to go out and pay for one of these sophisticated tests. A glance at the Weight Chart (table 2) and the use of the pinch-an-inch test can give you a general idea if you're overweight. If you decide to join a health club or gym, a good facility should

TABLE 2
Optimum Weight by Height and Frame Size

This table lists the range of weights that correlate with maximum life span, according to studies by the Metropolitan Life Insurance Company. To make an approximation of your frame size, extend your arm and bend the forearm upward at a 90-degree angle. Keep the palm turned toward your body and the fingers straight. If you have a caliper, use it to measure the space between the two prominent bones on either side of your elbow. Without a caliper, place the thumb and index finger of your other hand on those two bones. Measure the space between your fingers against a ruler or tape measure. Compare the measurement with the listings shown below for medium-framed men and women. Measurements lower than those listed indicate you have a small frame; higher measurements indicate a large frame.

MEN

Height without shoes	Elbow breadth
5′1″–5′2″	2½″–2⅞″
5′3″–5′6″	2⅝″–2⅞″
5′7″–5′10″	2¾″–3″
5′11″–6′2″	2¾″–3⅛″
6′3″	2⅞″–3¼″

WOMEN

Height without shoes	Elbow breadth
4′9″–4′10″	2¼″–2½″
4′11″–5′2″	2¼″–2½″
5′3″–5′6″	2⅜″–2⅝″
5′7″–5′10″	2⅜″–2⅝″
5′11″	2½″–2¾″

MEN — Height without shoes, weight without clothing

Height	Small frame	Medium frame	Large frame
5′1″	123–129 lbs.	126–136 lbs.	133–145 lbs.
5′2″	125–131	128–138	135–148
5′3″	127–133	130–140	137–151
5′4″	129–135	132–143	139–155
5′5″	131–137	134–146	141–159
5′6″	133–140	137–149	144–163
5′7″	135–143	140–152	147–167
5′8″	137–146	143–155	150–171
5′9″	139–149	146–158	153–175
5′10″	141–152	149–161	156–179
5′11″	144–155	152–165	159–183
6′0″	147–159	155–169	163–187
6′1″	150–163	159–173	167–192
6′2″	153–167	162–177	171–197
6′3″	157–171	166–182	176–202

WOMEN	Height without shoes, weight without clothing		
	Small frame	Medium frame	Large frame
4'9"	99–108 lbs.	106–108 lbs.	115–128 lbs.
4'10"	100–110	108–120	117–131
4'11"	101–112	110–123	119–134
5'0"	103–115	112–126	122–137
5'1"	105–118	115–129	125–140
5'2"	108–121	118–132	128–144
5'3"	111–124	121–135	131–148
5'4"	114–127	124–138	134–152
5'5"	117–130	127–141	137–156
5'6"	120–133	130–144	140–160
5'7"	123–136	133–147	143–164
5'8"	126–139	136–150	146–167
5'9"	129–142	139–153	149–170
5'10"	132–145	142–156	152–173

include a hydrostatic or skinfold caliper test free of charge as part of its assessment of your general fitness.

Muscular Strength   Your ability to lift a heavy suitcase gives you some idea of your muscular strength. To measure your total body strength, you must test all your major muscle groups. If you can pass the following four tests, you have a minimal level of muscular strength.

1. *Bent-knee sit-up.* For instructions on how to do a sit-up correctly, see page 57. If you have a history of lower-back problems, do not take this test without a physician's advice. You pass this test of minimal abdominal strength if you can do one sit-up without having your feet held down.

2. *Back and hip extension.* Do not take this test without a physician's advice if you have a history of lower-back problems. Lie facedown with a pillow under your waist, hands clasped behind your neck. While someone holds your legs down, lift your head and shoulders from the floor. Hold this position for ten seconds.

Then, with your hands on the floor and your upper body held down, lift your legs, keeping your knees straight. Breathe steadily; do not hold your breath. Hold this position ten seconds. You pass this test of minimal back strength if you can hold each movement for at least ten

seconds without straining.

3. *Full deep knee bend.* If you have had a severe knee injury, omit this test. Do one full deep knee bend and return to the standing position. Your heels can leave the floor. You pass this test of minimal leg strength if you can do one complete deep knee bend.

4. *Push-up.* For instructions on how to do a push-up correctly, see page 51. Remember to keep your back straight. You pass this test of minimal shoulder, chest, and arm strength if you can do one push-up correctly.

If you cannot pass these tests of minimal strength, you will need to undertake a program of weight training or calisthenics such as those described in chapters 3 and 4.

Muscular Endurance   Your level of muscular endurance depends in part on your level of muscular strength. It takes muscular strength to lift a heavy suitcase, but it takes muscular endurance to carry it from the car to the airport terminal.

The following two-part test will give you a general indication of your level of muscular endurance. The sit-up test measures abdominal endurance; the push-up test measures shoulder, chest, and arm endurance. If you have a history of back problems, do not undertake the first part of this test.

First, do as many bent-knee sit-ups as you can

TABLE 3
Muscular Endurance: Sit-up Test Evaluation

Age	Excellent	Very Good	Good	Fair	Poor
FEMALE					
15–29	More than 43	39–43	33–38	29–32	Less than 29
30–39	More than 35	31–35	25–30	21–24	Less than 21
40–49	More than 30	26–30	19–25	16–18	Less than 16
50–59	More than 25	21–25	15–20	11–14	Less than 11
60–69	More than 20	16–20	10–15	6–9	Less than 6
MALE					
15–29	More than 47	43–47	37–42	33–36	Less than 33
30–39	More than 39	35–39	29–34	25–28	Less than 25
40–49	More than 34	30–34	24–29	20–23	Less than 20
50–59	More than 29	25–29	19–24	15–18	Less than 15
60–69	More than 24	20–24	14–19	10–13	Less than 10

TABLE 4
Muscular Endurance: Push-up Test Evaluation

Age	Excellent	Very Good	Good	Fair	Poor
FEMALE					
15–29	More than 48	34–48	17–33	6–16	Less than 6
30–39	More than 39	25–39	12–24	4–11	Less than 4
40–49	More than 34	20–34	8–19	3–7	Less than 3
50–59	More than 29	15–29	6–14	2–5	Less than 2
60–69	More than 19	5–19	3–4	1–2	0
MALE					
15–29	More than 54	45–54	35–44	20–34	Less than 20
30–39	More than 44	35–44	25–34	15–24	Less than 15
40–49	More than 39	30–39	20–29	12–19	Less than 12
50–59	More than 34	25–34	15–24	8–14	Less than 8
60–69	More than 29	20–29	10–19	5–9	Less than 5

in 60 seconds. (For instructions, see page 57.) Rest one minute, then see how many consecutive push-ups you can do. Only count push-ups done with correct form. Women can do modified push-ups, which are the same as regular push-ups except they're done from the knees. (For instructions, see page 51.)

Use tables 3 and 4 to assess your muscular endurance. If you scored poorly, weight training or calisthenics can help build your muscular endurance. Chapters 3 and 4 can show you how to develop a program.

Flexibility Flexibility refers to your ability to move a joint through its full range of motion. Although flexibility can't be measured by a single exercise, this test of hamstring flexibility can give you a general idea of how limber you are.

First, place a foot-long strip of adhesive tape on the floor. Sit on the floor with your heels at the edge of the tape and your feet about five inches apart. Position a yardstick on the floor between your legs so that the one-inch mark is at the end closest your body and the 15-inch mark touches the edge of the tape. Keep your legs straight and *slowly* reach forward as far as you can without straining. Do not force the movement or bounce. Breathe regularly and deeply. Check the yardstick and note the distance you've reached. A distance of more than 15 inches means you've reached beyond your heel line.

Use table 5 to assess your hamstring flexibility, which is a good indication of total body flexibility. Regular stretching, done correctly, can gradually increase your flexibility.

	TABLE 5 **Flexibility Evaluation**				
	Excellent	Very Good	Good	Fair	Poor
Female	23 +"	21–23"	17–20"	13–16"	Below 13"
Male	21 +	19–21	14–18	12–13	Below 12

2

Goals and Expectations

About half the people who start exercise programs stop within the first six months, often because they have unreasonable expectations. No program can guarantee that you will be able to run a five-minute mile or complete a marathon. If you follow a sensible exercise program consistently, however, you'll find that overall fitness is more attainable than you probably realized.

To become fit, you need to exercise consistently and hard enough to make a difference. Although you might think that a few sets of tennis every Saturday are enough to keep you fit, most participatory sports are not taxing enough to contribute much to overall fitness, and weekend workouts are not frequent enough to keep your cardiovascular system in shape.

Performance Goals

Before you develop an exercise program, you need to take time to set specific performance goals. Use the results of the five-point fitness test in chapter 1 as a guide when setting your goals. If you earned a low score in the modified step test, if you need to lose fat or strengthen your heart, or if you want to lower your cholesterol level, you'll need to do aerobic exercise. The fundamentals of aerobic exercise are outlined in chapter 3, and several sample workouts are listed in chapter 4.

If your scores on the fitness tests show you need

to build muscle strength or muscle endurance, you can benefit from a weight-training or calisthenic program such as those described on page 25. If you need to increase your flexibility, you should pay special attention to the warm-up and cool-down stretches outlined in chapter 5.

Selected Performance Goals

Improve fitness test scores
Lose fat and body weight
Strengthen heart, improve cardiovascular
  fitness
Lower heart rate
Lower cholesterol level
Increase ratio of high-density lipoprotein (HDL)
  to low-density lipoprotein (LDL) cholesterol
Train for a sport
Relax
Reduce the effects of stress
Prevent injury
Acquire energy and stamina for day-to-day
  tasks
Develop a greater sense of well-being
Improve personal health
Acquire more energy and strength for hobbies
  and outside activities
Compete in an amateur athletic event
Manage pain, or recover from illness or injury
  (in conjunction with professional medical
  supervision only)

You may have other personal objectives in mind when deciding on an exercise program. You may want to get in condition so you can get through the day without feeling tired and run-down. Regular exercise can increase your energy level and help relieve the effects of a stressful workday.

Regular exercise can also help prevent injury and help you recover if you have been injured. When you're in condition, you're less likely to pull a muscle or strain a ligament.

After you have designed your workout routine, commit yourself to follow it for at least six weeks. If you stay with it for a month or more, you'll begin to feel the benefits of fitness and you'll be more likely to continue exercising. To get the full benefit of the physiological and metabolic changes that occur during exercise, you'll have to keep to your program for four to six months.

Remember, you didn't get out of shape in a few weeks, and you won't get into shape in a few weeks.

1. Set an overall performance goal.
2. Exercise regularly three times a week, or every other day. Commit yourself to your program and your goal.
3. Don't overdo. Start slowly, and gradually increase the intensity of your workout.
4. Keep your overall goal in mind as a motivator.

If you work out regularly and don't increase your food intake, you'll notice improvements in your body shape in roughly four to six weeks. It will take from six to 12 weeks to condition your body aerobically, provided you follow the aerobic fitness formula discussed in detail in chapter 3:

Despite the substantial advantages of exercise, it is not without risk. If you exercise only occasionally, you face a greater risk of injury than people who exercise regularly. "Weekend warriors" tend to push themselves too hard, and they often don't take time to prepare for exercise by warming up and stretching adequately.

If you exercise too much, you're also more prone to injuries, such as pulled muscle, strains, sprains, heat exhaustion, and sometimes even heart attack. Cases of sudden death from heart attacks during exercise are well documented, but there's no evidence that there is any additional risk of

---

Tips for Exercise Success

1. Select activities that interest you. Find a few activities you enjoy and vary them so you don't get bored. If you like the activity, you'll look forward to your workouts.

2. Set realistic performance goals for your program. Always start out doing less than you think you can; give your body time to adjust to a regular exercise routine. If you're not sure you can jog a mile, start by walking a mile or less. Do what you can, and slowly increase the intensity of your workout. Don't set unrealistic or impossible goals.

3. Exercise with a friend. If you have a partner, you might feel more inclined to stick to your routine on days when you feel like skipping your workout.

4. Make it a point to exercise whenever you can. Climb the stairs instead of taking the elevator. Walk to the bus stop instead of driving, or take a walk at lunchtime. Use a bicycle to run errands. These little changes can add up to real fitness benefits.

5. Make exercise an unconditional part of your daily or weekly schedule. Consistency counts. If you miss a few days of exercise, don't feel guilty and don't give up. Just get back into your routine the next day. Don't try to make up for lost time.

6. If you miss workouts for one week, cut back on the intensity of your workout and build up to the more intense routines. Don't pick up where you left off. You start to lose conditioning if you lay off your aerobic routine for as little as one week.

7. Keep exercising when you're away on vacation or business; don't take a sabbatical from your program. A growing number of hotels have in-house spas, gyms, and aerobic exercise classes. Many others have contracts with local health clubs that permit hotel guests to visit at little or no charge. Pack exercise shoes and clothes.

---

heart attack from exercising regularly. If you have heart problems, or if you're at risk of developing heart disease, check with your doctor before starting any exercise program.

As long as you warm up and cool down thoroughly and follow the few basic rules of exercise outlined in chapter 3, you should be able to enjoy a lifetime of exercise without excessive health risks.

Exercise Myths and Realities

Exercise has a folklore replete with myths, misinformation, and misconceptions—much of it passed around in locker rooms, gyms, and spas.

One of the most often heard maxims about exercise—and one that is not only false but dangerous—is "no pain, no gain." You do not have to suffer pain to improve your level of fitness. You do have to overload your muscles to make them stronger. This can cause an uncomfortable burning sensation as you work your muscles to exhaustion, but discomfort is not pain. If you're in pain, ease up.

The concept of "spot reduction" is another long-lived and over-hyped exercise myth. Some people try to flatten their stomachs by doing 100 sit-ups a day, and eventually quit in despair. Spot reduction does not work. In a sense, fat belongs to the entire body, not just the area where it's stored. When you exercise, you use fat from all over your body. Toning exercises can build muscle in a specific area, but they cannot make specific fat deposits disappear. If you're overweight, the best way to lose weight is to do any kind of aerobic exercise *and* to diet.

Many people, particularly sedentary people, still think that if you exercise regularly and then stop, your muscle will turn into fat. This is simply not true. A muscle cell is a muscle cell, and a fat cell is a fat cell. If you're physically active and you stop exercising, your muscle cells may decrease in size, but they will not become fat cells. For the same reason, exercise does not turn fat into muscle, another popular misconception. Fat takes up a great deal more space than does muscle. When you lose fat, you lose body mass.

A substantial number of bodybuilders believe that eating protein helps build muscles. In fact, if you eat a well-balanced diet, you consume all the protein necessary for vigorous training and muscle-building. Your body simply converts excess calories in the form of protein to fat and stores it in subcutaneous deposits.

Many women avoid weightlifting programs because they believe that they will develop big muscles. In fact, most women cannot build big muscles even when they try. Women have relatively low levels of testosterone, the hormone that affects muscle size. Unless a woman takes anabolic steroids, she is not likely to develop large muscles. Often, women weightlifters appear muscular because they have so little fat that their muscles can be seen better.

Other would-be weightlifters stay out of the weight room because they assume they will lose flexibility if they develop muscle bulk. Wrong again. Regular stretching can improve muscle flexibility, regardless of muscle size. Weight training, if done through the full range of motion, can actually enhance flexibility. But supplemental stretching is always recommended for weight trainers.

Another popular misconception is that exercise increases appetite. Unless you exercise strenuously for more than one hour, you're unlikely to experience any increase in appetite owing to exercise. When you exercise, your body temperature rises, which actually reduces the hormonal signal for hunger.

Many exercise enthusiasts also believe that cellulite is a special kind of fat. Actually, fat is fat, regardless of what it looks like. Cellulite probably gets its characteristic orange-peel appearance from the connective tissues that separate fat into compartments. When fat cells are full, the compartments bulge. Women tend to develop more cellulite than men do because they have thinner skin and larger, more rounded fat compartments.

The Benefits of Exercise

No matter how hard you work out, exercise can't overcome the effects of bad nutrition and family medical history. If you've inherited high cholesterol, diabetes, or heart disease, there's no guarantee that exercise can eliminate these problems, but in many cases it can help. Exercise isn't an antidote for harmful habits such as cigarette smoking or overeating, but a moderate, well-rounded fitness program that includes aerobic exercise at least three times a week can dramatically improve your overall health.

1. Exercise makes your heart a more efficient pump, thereby lowering blood pressure. Exercise also increases the size and number of mitochondria—energy-producing organelles within body cells that are also responsible for cell respiration—enabling your muscles to extract oxygen from your blood more easily.

2. Aerobic exercise can help promote healthy arteries by reducing triglyceride and sometimes total cholesterol levels. It increases the level of high-density lipoproteins in the blood, which may help remove artery-damaging cholesterol. Body chemistry differs from person to person. Some people who exercise and follow low-cholesterol diets still can't overcome problems of high cholesterol, but exercise helps many people control their cholesterol levels.

3. Exercise may help you live a longer, more productive life. A long-term study of 17,000 Harvard alumni concluded that a person who burns 2,000 calories or more per week in moderate exercise will probably live longer than someone who doesn't exercise. Although debate over the methods and conclusions of the longevity studies continues, most researchers agree that the health benefits of exercise can improve the quality of life for the years you live, if they don't actually add years to your life.

4. Exercise may help to reduce the effects of stress, easing muscle tension, increasing blood circulation, and lowering blood pressure. Also, the more physically fit you are, the better you can withstand stress.

5. Exercise can help you lose weight and keep it off. Increased activity burns calories and speeds up your metabolism both during exercise and afterward.

6. Exercise may lower the chance of breast and reproductive-system cancers in women, according to a continuing study at Harvard University of 5,000 graduates of ten colleges and universities.

7. Exercise helps some diabetics increase their bodies' sensitivity to insulin, the hormone that removes excess sugar from the bloodstream. It can reduce the insulin requirement for some diabetics, and can sometimes eliminate the need for insulin entirely, according to research done by Dr. James Anderson at the University of Kentucky.

8. Exercise during pregnancy can help increase energy, control weight gain, prepare the body for labor, and improve blood circulation, which can help prevent stagnation of blood and the formation of varicose veins.

9. Exercise is one of the most important measures you can take to help forestall osteoporosis, a disease characterized by excessive loss of bone density that makes the skeleton abnormally fragile. Although all adults lose bone as they age, once bone is lost, it can't be replenished. For the present, the best approach is preventive, and exercise is vital for preserving bone. Even light to moderate exercise can increase bone density. Not all types of exercise are equally helpful in building bone, however. The best exercises appear to be weight-bearing ones such as walking, jogging, aerobics, rope-jumping, and practically any sport that gets you to move around. Swimming may not be as effective as landlocked exercise, because your weight is mostly supported by water.

10. Prolonged exercise can cause the release of beta-endorphins, a hormone known to ease the symptoms of depression. These beta-endorphins also cause a feeling of well-being or euphoria, known as runner's high, that some endurance athletes experience after exercising half an hour or more.

11. Exercise can help you stop smoking. Smokers who exercise regularly often quit because smoking decreases lung capacity and makes it harder to breathe during exercise. (Nicotine does not prevent the conditioning effects of exercise. Therefore, smokers who exercise are still better off than those who don't.) If you're a smoker, one of the best things you can do for your health is to quit. Smokers are three times more likely to have heart attacks than are non-smokers. Nevertheless, an ex-smoker's risk of heart attack drops to normal two years after he or she kicks the habit, according to a study done by the Boston University School of Medicine.

3

Fitness Fundamentals

The human body has an amazing ability to adapt to physical demands. If you follow a sensible exercise program, your body will respond to the increased demands you make on it, and you will become more fit. Developing an effective, safe, and enjoyable program is not as difficult as you might think. All you must do is follow a few simple rules and remember the two basic principles of training: specificity and progressive overload.

Specificity and Progressive Overload

Specificity simply means that your exercise program should be designed to meet your personal goals. Review your scores on the fitness assessment tests in chapter 1 and your performance goals, and consider which areas you need and want to work on. The programs described in chapter 4 can help you choose a fitness routine to meet your needs.

Progressive overload means gradually pushing your body past its normal work load. If you're not accustomed to lifting anything heavier than a ten-pound bag of groceries, you'll find it difficult to lift a 20-pound barbell. You probably could lift the heavier weight, but your muscles would strain slightly and your heart rate would increase. If you continued to lift the heavier weight, your body would adjust; your muscles would become stronger and your heart and lungs would learn to work more efficiently. In a couple of weeks, you could do the work with less exertion. The principle of

progressive overload applies equally to building aerobic fitness, muscular strength and endurance, and flexibility. You can overload your muscles in three ways:

1. by increasing exercise *intensity,* for example the amount of weight you lift or rate you run
2. by increasing exercise *duration,* the length of time you lift the weight, run, or stretch
3. by increasing exercise *frequency,* the number of times per week you exercise

The rule for success and for safety is to work slowly and consistently. You should increase your work load by no more than 10 percent per week. Give your body time to adjust to your fitness program.

Aerobic Fitness: Working in the Exercise Benefit Zone

The term *aerobic* means "using oxygen." During aerobic exercise, your heart and lungs work harder than normal to provide your muscles with the oxygen they need. You work at a slow and steady pace—hard enough to get you breathing heavily, but not hard enough to leave you gasping for breath. Aerobic exercise is the most important component of a fitness program.

Sudden bursts of activity, such as sprinting for the bus or spiking a volleyball, are *anaerobic,* which means you're exercising so hard that your muscles demand more oxygen than your body can provide. That's why sprinters gasp for breath at the end of a race. No one can do anaerobic exercise for more than a couple of minutes, but everyone can and should do aerobic exercise for extended periods.

To improve aerobic fitness and strengthen your heart and lungs, you need to choose an aerobic exercise program that uses your large muscle groups steadily and rhythmically. Activities like walking, jogging, bicycling, swimming, cross-country skiing, aerobic dancing, and rope-skipping are good choices.

Aerobic exercise doesn't strengthen your cardiovascular system unless the workout is intense enough to raise your heart rate above its resting level for at least 20 minutes. You don't need to raise it to the maximum, just to about 60 percent of maximum. Seventy percent of maximum is a good *target heart rate* for many people. You should, of course, check with your doctor, particularly if you're middle-aged or older, but you can improve your aerobic fitness by exercising at as low as 45 percent of your maximum heart rate. Working at 60 to 70 percent of maximum is simply more efficient for the average person. Athletes and people in very good condition might want to start at 70 percent and work up to 85 percent of maximum.

To determine whether or not you're working hard enough, you should monitor your heart rate. You can take your pulse at either your radial artery (in your wrist, just inside your wristbone) or your carotid artery (on the side of your throat, under your jawbone, about midway between your chin and ear). As a good practice, take your pulse at the radial artery. Taking the pulse at the carotid artery can cause dizziness, fainting, and can elevate diastolic blood pressure; it's not recommended, particularly for older people. The illustration on page 13 shows the location of the radial artery. Hold your fingers firmly in place to feel the artery pulsating. Each pulsation indicates a single heartbeat.

To find your pulse rate, use a stopwatch or a watch with a sweep second hand to time yourself as you count the number of heartbeats in ten seconds, then multiply the number by six.

You should try to work in your *exercise benefit zone,* 60 to 85 percent of your maximum heart rate. If you work in this zone, your aerobic fitness will improve and you will burn fat. If you work beyond the benefit zone, you will start doing anaerobic exercise, meaning you can't keep up the pace too long.

Use table 6 to determine your exercise benefit zone. To build and maintain aerobic fitness and strengthen your cardiovascular system you need to exercise 20 to 30 minutes at 60 to 85 percent of your maximum heart rate at least three times a week. (A good target heart rate for most people is about 70 percent.) If you exercise less often or less intensely, your cardiovascular fitness won't improve and you will lose conditioning.

When you're getting started, take your heart rate at least twice during exercise. Slow down if you're working above the exercise benefit zone. If you're working below the zone, pick up the pace. With practice, you can better judge whether or not you're working near your target heart rate without stopping to take your pulse.

Taking your pulse at the radial artery
Use the index and middle fingers of either hand and press quite firmly, but without causing pain, beside the outside bone (radius) of your forearm, just below the wrist joint of the opposite hand.

It's important to consider how you feel on a particular day. Don't become a slave to your stopwatch. Ease off of your planned routine if you're feeling the effects of temperature, humidity, or altitude, or if you're feeling worn down by fatigue, stress, or illness.

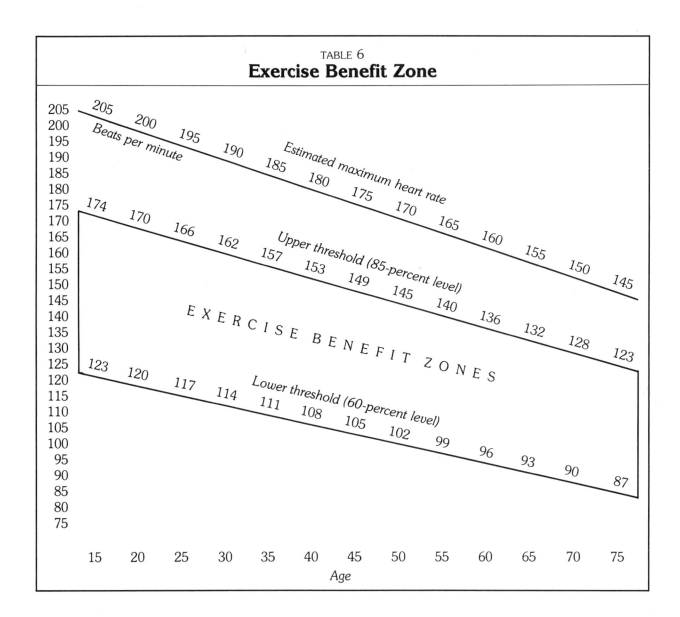

TABLE 6
Exercise Benefit Zone

After aerobic exercise, it takes a few minutes for your breathing and pulse rate to return to normal. Generally, the more fit you are, the faster your body will recover.

If you've been sedentary, it will take ten to twelve weeks to start gaining the benefits of aerobic conditioning and four to six months for your metabolism to change and to enjoy long-lasting benefits of exercise. Work out regularly; it can take as little as a week to lose much of your conditioning, depending on your fitness level. Follow these rules to exercise for aerobic fitness:

1. Exercise 20 to 30 minutes

2. at 60 to 85 percent of your maximum heart rate

3. at least three times a week or every other day

Body Composition: Losing Fat, Not Muscle

Your body is made up of muscle, bone, and fat. Techniques such as underwater weighing and caliper-pinch tests can be used to determine just how fat—or lean—you are, but these tests require specialized equipment that may not be available to you. The self-assessment test in chapter 2 can give you a rough idea of whether or not you're overly fat. Don't be afraid of all fat. Your body needs a certain amount of stored fat to function properly; acceptable rates are about 15 to 20 percent body fat for men and about 20 to 25 percent for women. You should be concerned with *excess* fat, which has been linked to heart disease, diabetes, gallbladder disease, and high blood pressure.

Though you've heard it before, the only effective way to control your weight is to exercise regularly and eat a balanced diet. To lose weight, you have to use more calories through exercise or activity than you consume in the foods you eat. To lose one pound of body fat, you must spend about 3,500 calories, the equivalent of well over five hours of vigorous aerobic exercise for the average-sized man or woman.

The best way to lose fat is to eat less and exercise more. Dieting alone can make you lose muscle as well as fat, but a combination of diet and exercise will help you tone muscle while you lose fat. Strengthening muscle actually helps you lose weight more quickly because it takes more energy for your body to work muscle than to burn fat. About 90 percent of the calories you use each day are consumed by muscle, even when you're not exercising.

No matter how hard you exercise or how much you diet, you can't get rid of fat cells. When you lose weight, your fat cells become smaller, but they don't disappear. To shrink your fat cells and lose weight, you should do aerobic exercise. Anaerobic exercise does not burn fat. Brief, high-intensity anaerobic exercise uses muscle glycogen as fuel. Glycogens are the carbohydrate reserves stored in the muscles as sugar. During aerobic exercise, your body uses fat. Obviously, the more frequently and the longer you exercise, the more calories you'll burn.

Don't assume you'll use more calories by doing a high-intensity exercise. If you do a low-intensity exercise for a longer time, you may burn more calories than by doing a high-intensity exercise for a shorter time. For example, you may actually use more calories in walking an hour than you would by jogging for 20 minutes.

Remember, the best way to lose fat is through a combination of balanced diet and aerobic exercise. Table 8, on page 20, can help you find an exercise that uses a lot of calories.

Muscular Strength and Endurance: Working Harder for Longer

The only way to increase strength and endurance is to overload your muscles *gradually*. The best way to do this is to follow a weight-training program. You can use free weights or weight machines for resistance, or you can do calisthenics and work against your own body weight.

When used, muscles go through two types of contractions. The first, *concentric contractions,* do positive work, as is done in the upward motion of a bicep curl. The second, *eccentric contractions,* do negative work, as is done when lowering the weight during a bicep curl. Concentric contractions shorten your muscles, and eccentric contractions lengthen them. It's important to do both types of work when exercising to stabilize your muscles and keep them in balance.

Some people who weightlift do "negatives": they have a trainer lift a weight, then they lower it using an eccentric contraction. This negative work helps lengthen muscles, which can make them work more efficiently. It can also cause additional muscle soreness.

If you want to exercise for strength and endurance, you will have to do one of three types of exercise:

1. *Isotonics.* Bench pressing a barbell or doing a push-up is an example of isotonic exercise. During isotonic exercise, the weight lifted or pushed against remains constant, while the effort provided by the muscle varies from maximum in the muscle's weakest range of motion to moderate in the muscle's strongest range of motion.
2. *Isometrics.* In doing isometrics, you push against an immovable resistance, for example, standing in a doorway and pushing against the frame as hard as you can. Isometric exercises strengthen the muscles at only one point in their range of motion.

3. *Isokinetics.* Machines that provide true isokinetic exercise are extremely expensive and complex. You are unlikely to encounter one outside of a physical therapy facility. Only isokinetic machines exercise a muscle to its maximum through its full range of motion. Isokinetic machines provide muscular overload using a motor preset at a speed and programmed to adjust to the differences in strength at different points in the muscle. Thus, the muscle can exert 100-percent effort at each point through its range of motion.

You can adjust the amount of weight you lift to build either muscular strength, muscular endurance, or both. To build strength, lift the heaviest weight you can for six to eight repetitions of an exercise, doing two or three sets of each exercise. When you can do two or three sets of eight repetitions, increase the weight and return to six repetitions. To build endurance, follow the same overload principle, but use a lighter weight that allows you to do one set of 10 to 20 repetitions. To build both strength and endurance, do one set of 8 to 15 repetitions with moderate weight before increasing the weight. When you start out, begin with less weight and *gradually* increase it to increase your work load.

The limits to your muscular strength depend on the size and type of muscle fibers you were born with. Muscles are made up of *fast-twitch* and *slow-twitch fibers.* Generally, the more fast-twitch fibers you have, the better you are at explosive bursts of anaerobic activity, like sprinting. The more slow-twitch fibers you have, the better you are at aerobic endurance exercise. You can't do much to change the number of fast-twitch or slow-twitch fibers in your muscles; the ratio of fast to slow fibers is genetically determined. You can increase the size of one type of fiber over the other by exercising them.

For more information on weight-training programs, see page 25.

Flexibility: Stretching for Suppleness and to Prevent Injury

Your flexibility depends on the condition of your bones, tendons, ligaments, and muscles. Joints that are regularly moved through their full range of motion retain their normal mobility, while those that aren't become less supple. Flexibility not only permits freedom of movement, but it also makes you less prone to many injuries such as muscle pulls, strains, and tears.

To improve flexibility, you must stretch regularly. This is especially important if your fitness program includes an exercise that doesn't take a joint through its full range of motion. Jogging, for example, can tighten the hamstrings, the hip flexors that bring your leg forward, the Achilles tendons in the calves, and the quadriceps in the upper thigh. Joggers can maintain—and even gain—flexibility in these muscles if they stretch them regularly. Just as with aerobic fitness activities, every fitness routine should include some stretching.

The exercises listed in the warm-up section of chapter 5 can help you get started on a stretching program.

4

Choosing an Exercise Program

Every well-rounded exercise program includes some form of regular aerobic exercise to strengthen the cardiovascular system. When it comes to fitness, it doesn't matter how slim or muscular you are; you're not really in shape until your heart and lungs are in shape.

This chapter describes some of the most popular options for people who want to build cardiovascular fitness and lose weight. In most cases, the programs don't require any special skills. If you try one type of exercise and find, after a reasonable time, that you don't like it, switch to another. Find two or more kinds of exercise you enjoy, and vary your routine, a technique known as *cross training*.

Fitness Guidelines

Whatever exercise you choose for the aerobic portion of your workout, follow these five fitness guidelines:

1. Begin every workout with a warm-up and end every workout with a cool-down. See the warm-up section of chapter 5 for a list of suggested stretches.
2. Work within your exercise benefit zone at 60 to 85 percent of your maximum heart rate. Use your pulse rate to guide the intensity of your workout.
3. Exercise continuously for 20 to 30 minutes.
4. Work out three or four times a week, every other day. You don't need to work out every day, but if you plan to exercise on consecutive days, be sure to alternate between two or more activities that use different muscle groups. Doing several types of exercise helps avoid muscle imbalance and overuse.
5. As your fitness level improves, gradually increase the intensity, duration, or frequency of your workouts. Follow the 10-percent rule: Increase the intensity or duration of exercise by no more than 10 percent per week.

Overtraining

If you allow yourself proper breaks between workouts, you'll gain strength faster and with less risk of injury. Don't be so eager to see results that you overwork yourself. Your body needs its rest. Watch for the signs of overtraining:

- increased nervousness or depression
- inability to relax or to sleep
- desire to quit training
- extreme soreness and stiffness the day after a workout
- gradual increase in soreness from one workout to the next
- unexplained weight loss
- increase in your resting heart rate
- rundown feeling
- loss of appetite
- constipation or diarrhea
- unexplained drop in performance

If you're overtraining, give yourself a break. Cut back on the intensity, duration, or frequency of your routine for two or three workouts or until you feel like pushing yourself again.

Choosing Activities to Meet Your Goals

Before choosing an exercise program, consider your fitness goals. Table 7 can help you decide if the activities in your fitness routine will help you reach those goals. The table rates a number of popular exercises and activities on their ability to improve aerobic fitness, body composition, muscle strength, muscle endurance, and flexibility.

Your exercise program should include activities rated high enough in aerobic fitness that you can exercise for 20 to 30 minutes at 60 to 85 percent of your maximum heart rate. Some activities, such as yoga or horseback riding, do not meet this aerobic fitness standard, but they can supplement your regular aerobic program. In addition to the usual warm-up and cool-down stretching, it's a good idea to do some extra stretching regularly, on days between workouts, for example.

Counting Calories

If you want to lose weight, include in your routine an exercise that burns a lot of calories. The number of calories burned per hour varies among individuals, depending on body weight, metabolism, intensity of exercise, clothing, and the weather. Tables 8 and 9 can give you a general idea of how many calories you burn performing different sport and nonsport activities.

Running or Jogging

Jogging is an excellent aerobic exercise, whether you do it in a park, at a track, or on a treadmill. For cardiovascular conditioning, jog so that your heart rate is in the exercise benefit zone for 20 to 30 minutes—three times a week. During your workouts, focus on the length of time you jog, not the distance you cover.

When you're just getting started, you might want to alternate brisk walks with slow jogs for a couple of weeks. For example, you could jog for two minutes and walk for two minutes. As your muscles, tendons, ligaments, and cardiovascular system adjust, then jog for longer time periods and walk for shorter ones.

If your goal is weight loss, keep in mind that you use about 100 calories per mile. The heavier you are, the more calories you burn per mile. Generally, as far as calories are concerned, it makes little difference how fast you run. You use about the same number of calories to run a mile in ten minutes as to run a mile in five minutes. You're burning roughly twice as many calories when you run faster, but you run the mile in half the time, so the energy cost per mile is about the same.

You can build muscular strength and endurance by running if you follow the basic principle of progressive overload. Work a little bit harder than you're used to, and you'll grow stronger. Follow the 10-percent rule: Increase your running time, mileage, or speed by no more than 10 percent per week.

Jogging does nothing to improve flexibility, and it can actually decrease flexibility in your quadriceps and Achilles tendons. To prevent injuries and knee problems, stretch your legs and hamstrings before and after running. You can use the warm-up and cool-down routines described in chapter 5. To help prevent shinsplints, ankle injury, and stress fractures, you should add a selection of the strengthening and stretching exercises described in the ''Shinsplints and Ankle Sprains'' section of chapter 8 to your warm-up and cooldown. To help prevent back strain, you can add a selection of exercises from the ''Lower-Back Pain'' section of the same chapter.

If you have knee or lower-back problems, talk to your doctor before starting a running program. If you don't have knee problems, moderate running for about 20 miles or less per week is not likely to hurt your knees. Avoid jogging on hard surfaces.

Keeping Pace   For aerobic training, most of the time you'll be running long, slow distances at a comfortable pace. You can alternate this distance training with interval training or *fartlek* runs to build speed or for a change of pace.

TABLE 7
Fitness Ratings for Popular Activities

Activity	Aerobic Fitness	Body Composition	Muscle Strength	Muscle Endurance	Flexibility
Aerobic exercise routines					
Low-impact	1	2	4	3	2
High-impact	1	1	2	1	2
Aqua stretching	5	4	4	4	1
Ballet	3	3	2	1	1
Ballroom dancing	3	4	2	1	1
Basketball	2	2	4	2	3
Bicycling					
13 mph	1	2	3	1	2
20 mph	1	1	2	1	2
Bowling	5	5	4	5	4
Calisthenic circuit training	1	1	3	1	3
Canoeing, kayaking	3	3	3	2	3
Cheerleading	3	3	3	3	2
Cross-country skiing	1	1	3	1	2
Dancing: folk, square	2	3	4	3	3
Dancing: rock 'n' roll	3	4	5	3	4
Field hockey	1	1	3	1	3
Football (touch)	4	4	4	4	4
Golf (carrying bag)	3	4	4	3	3
Handball (singles)	2	2	4	2	2
Hiking	1	2	3	2	5
Hockey (ice)	1	2	3	2	4
Horseback riding	4	4	4	4	5
Jogging/running					
12 min./mile	1	1	3	2	5
7 min./mile	1	1	2	1	5
sprinting	4	3	2	3	4
Karate	2	2	3	1	1
Racquetball	2	2	4	3	3
Rope jumping	1	2	4	2	4
Rowing	1	2	1	1	2
Sailing	5	5	5	4	5
Skateboarding	3	4	4	3	4
Skating (ice, roller)	2	3	3	2	3
Skiing (downhill)	3	3	2	2	4
Soccer	1	1	3	1	3
Swimming					
20 yd./min.	2	2	3	1	2
55 yd./min.	1	1	2	1	2
Tennis (singles)	3	3	4	3	3
Volleyball	3	3	5	4	3
Walking					
Brisk walking	1	2	3	4	3
Racewalking	1	1	2	2	4
Waterskiing	4	5	3	2	4
Weightlifting	5	3	1	2	2
Windsurfing	3	4	3	2	3
Yoga	5	4	5	3	1

Key: Excellent–1 Very Good–2 Good–3 Fair–4 Poor–5

TABLE 8
Calories Used per Hour of Sport Activity

Activity	100 lb.	120 lb.	150 lb.	180 lb.	200 lb.
Swimming (20 yd./min.)	192 per hr.	230 per hr.	288 per hr.	346 per hr.	384 per hr.
Tennis (beginner)	192	230	288	346	384
Canoeing (flat water/4 mph)	270	324	405	486	540
Golf (carrying clubs)	270	324	405	486	540
Table tennis (skilled)	270	324	405	486	540
Aerobic dance (low impact)	276	331	414	497	552
Walking (4.5 mph)	288	346	432	518	576
Touch football (moderate)	294	353	441	529	588
Backpacking (40-lb. pack)	312	374	468	562	624
Hockey (ice or field)	312	374	468	562	624
Horseback riding (trot)	312	374	468	562	624
Calisthenic circuit training	360	432	540	648	720
Jogging (5 mph)	360	432	540	648	720
Aerobic dancing (high impact)	372	446	558	670	744
Bicycling (13 mph)	426	511	639	767	852
Handball (skilled, singles)	468	562	702	842	936
Jumping rope (moderate)	474	569	711	853	948
Swimming (55 yd./min.)	528	634	792	950	1,056
Basketball (full/vigorous)	582	698	873	1,048	1,164
Rowing (vigorous)	582	698	873	1,048	1,164
Soccer (vigorous)	582	698	873	1,048	1,164
Cross-country skiing (8 mph)	624	749	936	1,123	1,248
Running (8 mph)	624	749	936	1,123	1,248

TABLE 9
Calories Used per Hour of Ordinary Activity

Activity	100 lb.	120 lb.	150 lb.	180 lb.	200 lb.
Eating	66 per hr.	79 per hr.	99 per hr.	119 per hr.	132 per hr.
Piano playing	108	130	162	194	216
Driving a car	120	144	180	216	240
Cleaning windows	144	173	216	259	288
Raking leaves	144	173	216	259	288
Mopping floors	144	173	216	259	288
Ironing	174	209	261	313	348
Bed-making/stripping	186	223	279	335	372
Weeding	228	274	342	410	456
Chopping wood	294	353	441	529	588
Snow shoveling	312	374	468	562	624
Sawing wood	348	418	522	626	696

Interval training lets you extend your workout by varying your pace for set time periods. Suppose you want to prepare for a five-mile race at an eight-mile-per-hour pace. You would run ten or more three-minute or half-mile intervals at the eight-mile-per-hour pace or better, then walk or jog a minute or until your heart rate falls below your benefit zone. You can vary the distance, pace, or number of intervals you do.

Fartlek is a Swedish word meaning "speed play." The technique can be useful to a conditioned runner. Normally, when you run long distances, your pace is steady. When you run fartleks, your pace is freewheeling and unpredictable. Do what you feel like doing; run as fast or as slow as you like for as long or as short a period as you choose, mixing sprints with walking. Fartleks can provide a welcome relief from the structure of steady distance training, but this type of training should not be undertaken by the novice runner.

Running Tips

• *Wear good running shoes and make sure they fit properly (see page 80). Your feet hit the ground about 1,000 times every mile, landing with a force equal to three to five times your body weight, therefore it's important to wear shoes with thick, well-padded soles that can absorb shock. A running shoe should also be flexible and provide heel support. Replace your shoes when the cushioning feels "dead" or when the heel counter becomes weak.*

• *Be sure to stretch before and after your run. Pay special attention to the hamstring, quadricep, and Achilles tendon stretches.*

• *Whenever possible, run on soft surfaces to help blunt the shock of hitting the ground.*

• *When running on the street, run against the flow of traffic, and wear reflective clothing.*

• *To increase speed, you must increase either the length of your stride or the number of strides you take in a minute, or both. It's usually best to take more strides, since longer strides are more tiring.*

• *If you need to lengthen your stride even though it can be tiring, for example when trying to improve your running speed, focus on pushing off harder with your back leg rather than reaching forward with your lead leg. (Lift your lead leg, rather than reaching with it.) You don't want your*

foot to land ahead of your center of gravity, or your leg muscles have to work to catch up before they can propel you forward.

• *When running uphill, shorten your stride and concentrate on lifting your knees and landing more toward the front of your foot. Pump your arms as if you were cross-country skiing.*

• *When running downhill, tilt your body forward to keep it perpendicular to the slope. Avoid barreling down the hill. Don't lean backward or you'll land hard on your heels.*

• *Avoid running pigeon-toed. This can cause shinsplints.*

• *If you want to train for a race, don't run too slowly. If you train at a slow pace, you'll race at a slow pace. Interval training can help you develop a faster pace.*

• *If you're going to be in a race, do one hard workout run about five to seven days before competition, then decrease your mileage. Take a day off before the race. If you aren't ready for a race by then, an extra training push just before race day won't help you.*

• *Be sure to take time to recover between races. As a general rule, allow enough time between races of about the same distance so that you can run regular workouts whose accumulated mileage equals ten times the race distance.*

• *Don't enter a 10-kilometer race until you can run about 20 miles a week for five weeks in a row without injury. Don't enter a marathon until you can do 35 to 40 miles of training a week for ten weeks without injury.*

• *Be sure your heels strike the ground first, then roll smoothly to your toes. Listen to your footsteps. If you hear your foot slap the ground, your form is wrong—you're running flat-footed.*

• *Keep your arms and hands relaxed but not floppy. Hold your forearms at right angles to your body, pumping straight ahead, not across the front of your torso.*

Walking

Walking is an excellent aerobic activity, no matter what your fitness level. It can be just as enriching as more strenuous activities, as long as you elevate your heart rate to your exercise benefit zone for 20 to 30 minutes at least three times a week.

Some people prefer walking to running because the gliding motion of walking reduces the amount of shock to the body. When walking, you don't become airborne during your stride as you do when running, so you don't have the impact when your feet hit the ground.

Walking can build muscle strength and endurance in your legs. You should walk briskly when walking for fitness, at a three-to-five-mile-per-hour pace while swinging your arms. Follow the same basic guidelines when developing a walking program as you would in developing a running or jogging program.

You can make brisk walking part of a weight-control program. You burn about the same number of calories walking a mile as you do jogging a mile; it just takes longer to walk.

Walking Tips

- *Maintain good posture while walking. Keep your head up, shoulders back, and chest out.*
- *Be sure to wear good walking shoes with adequate arch support.*
- *Stretch before you walk. Follow the stretches listed on pages 36–39 for a basic warm-up routine.*
- *Walk for time instead of mileage.*
- *Include hills in your route.*
- *If you must walk in the road, walk against the flow of traffic. Wear reflective clothing when walking at night.*
- *Walking isn't a high-risk activity, but you can injure your Achilles tendon if you overstride.*
- *If you want to burn more calories or increase your work load to get your heart rate up, you can:*
  —Walk up a hill
  —Climb some stairs
  —Pump your arms as you walk
  —Wear hand weights and swing your arms
  —Walk on the beach (You burn about twice as many calories walking in sand as walking on a hard surface. But be sure to stretch thoroughly. Walking on sand stresses the Achilles tendons and calves more than walking on a hard surface.)

Bicycling

Bicycling offers the same cardiovascular and strength-building benefits as running or walking, and it improves flexibility in the hips and legs as well. Biking is suitable for people of all ages and fitness levels, and it can be a good choice for the overweight because the seat bears most of the body's weight.

Even if you're a beginner, you can probably pedal a bike three times a week for 20 to 30 minutes in your exercise benefit zone. When you're getting started, riding at 12 to 15 miles per hour will usually be enough to get your heart rate sufficiently elevated. As you get stronger, you can increase the intensity of your workout by pedaling faster or, better yet, riding longer.

Select a gear that allows you to pedal about 80 to 90 revolutions per minute. Pedaling slower in a higher gear doesn't give you a better workout, it just increases the pressure and stress on your knees. *Spinning*, pedaling faster in a lower gear, is the best way to strengthen your heart. Spinning also reduces the chances of injury and minimizes fatigue.

Since you use the large quadricep muscles in your upper leg for cycling, make a point of thoroughly stretching these muscles. Hamstring and lower back stretches increase range of motion and also help prevent injury.

Beginning cyclists sometimes suffer from backache and neck strain. To prevent strain, pay special attention to stretching your back and neck muscles during your warm-up. Several stretches that you may find helpful are listed in chapter 5 and in the "Lower-Back Pain" section of chapter 8.

Be sure to pick a comfortable seat. After sitting for an extended period, your buttocks can become uncomfortable. Men sometimes have a tendency to develop prostatitis, an infection of the prostate gland. If your buttocks feel uncomfortable, periodically ride for a few minutes standing up on the pedals to give your buttocks a rest.

Your hands or fingers may feel numb or tingle after extended periods of gripping the handlebars. To relieve this discomfort, make it a point to shift your hands around frequently. You can also try using padded grips or gloves.

Bicycling Tips

• *Wear a hard helmet. Choose one approved by the American National Standards Institute or by the Snell Memorial Foundation.*
• *Use a bicycle light and wear reflective clothing if you ride at night.*
• *Always ride with the flow of traffic.*
• *Avoid wearing restrictive clothing and loose pants or skirts that can become caught in the chain.*
• *Keep your arms bent slightly to absorb shock; don't lock your elbows.*
• *Make sure your bike fits you. Adjust the seat so that when you're sitting squarely on the saddle with the balls of your feet on the pedals, the knee of your extended leg is bent at a 15- or 20-degree angle. Incorrect seat height can cause knee problems.*
• *Always pedal with the balls of your feet.*
• *To strengthen your legs and increase your speed, wear toe clips. They can significantly increase your pedaling efficiency because you can work on both pushing on the downstroke and pulling up on the upstroke. This allows you to use your hamstrings and calves, in addition to your quadriceps. One way to work these muscles even harder is to practice pedaling with one foot, alternating feet.*
• *To build speed, do interval training by increasing your speed for several minutes, then coasting until your heart rate slows down. Or you can pedal uphill and glide downhill.*

Swimming

Swimming is one of the most effective exercises you can include in your fitness program. Swimming involves all the major muscles in your body, so it's good for aerobic conditioning and weight control. It also builds strength and endurance in your legs and upper body and improves shoulder flexibility. The natural resistance of the water helps tone and strengthen your muscles.

Swimming is ideal for beginning exercisers, for people with certain orthopedic or health problems, and for the elderly, because the buoyancy provided by the water helps reduce pressure on your joints and bones. When you're in water, you weigh only 10 percent as much as you do on land, and your body weight is evenly distributed.

When you begin your program, start at a pace that's comfortable, and use whatever strokes enable you to complete your workout. Concentrate on breathing regularly, which will enable you to swim without resting frequently. If you get tired, switch strokes or rest briefly between laps.

Try to swim for 20 to 30 minutes with your heart rate elevated into the exercise benefit zone. Use interval training (page 21) if you cannot swim 20 to 30 minutes straight. (You could, for example, swim for five minutes and rest for one.) Your maximum heart rate is about 13 beats per minute slower when you're swimming than when you're doing other exercises, probably in part because your body is horizontal and your heart doesn't have to pump blood against gravity. In addition, when you're swimming, your heart can pump more blood with each heartbeat. The fact that your body can more efficiently transfer heat to the water may also help lower your heart rate.

When using table 6 on page 14 to determine whether or not you're working in your exercise

Swimming Tips

• *Breathe rhythmically by coordinating your strokes and your breathing. Don't fight the water. Use your breathing to relax "into" the water; this will, in fact, make you more buoyant and make you feel more confident. If you're uncomfortable in the water, consider taking swimming lessons from a local recreation facility or "Y" organization.*
• *Stretch before and after swimming. The warmup routine outlined in chapter 5 or the underwater stretches on pages 27–35 can help.*
• *In general, women make better swimmers than men. This is partly because most women have more body fat than men and are therefore more buoyant.*
• *If you have lower-back problems, avoid the breaststroke and crawl, or mix strokes so you don't overuse the lower-back muscles.*
• *Kickboards, hand paddles, and fins can help you isolate certain muscle groups during your workout. Kickboards and fins work your legs, and hand paddles exercise your arms and shoulders.*

benefit zone, subtract 13 from the "beats per minute" numbers.

The most common strokes in swimming are the crawl or freestyle, which builds the quadriceps, shoulders, and calves; the sidestroke, which builds quadriceps, calves, and ankles; the backstroke, which builds the back, quadriceps, and abdomen; and the breaststroke, which builds the upper body and inner thighs. The breaststroke is the least efficient stroke, and the freestyle is the most efficient. Use any combination of these strokes in your workout. It's best to vary your strokes. That way you can swim longer and work several different muscle groups.

Aerobic Exercise Classes

An aerobic exercise class consists of a routine of choreographed calisthenics—running, kicking, skipping, hopping, jumping, bending, and stretching, often performed to music. Most aerobic exercise classes or videotapes have warm-up and stretching routines, followed by strenuous aerobic activity, and ending with a slow cool-down routine. Some programs also include floor exercises designed to strengthen the upper body, abdominal, and hip muscles.

Aerobic exercise routines obviously provide excellent cardiovascular conditioning and are also good for muscle strength and endurance. If your aerobic program includes a period of warm-up and stretching, you'll also improve your flexibility.

To gain aerobic benefits, you have to follow the basic aerobic conditioning rules: Exercise 20 to 30 minutes a minimum of three times a week; work hard enough to get your heart rate up to 60 to 85 percent of its maximum. During your workout you should take at least one break to check your pulse. At this halfway point you can check your heart rate to see whether or not you're working in your exercise benefit zone, and decide whether you need to take it easy or push yourself.

There are two basic types of aerobic routines, high-impact and low-impact. During low-impact aerobic routines you keep one foot on the ground at all times to avoid the more jarring movements of high-impact aerobics. Some people prefer low-impact routines because they believe there's less chance of injury. Other people find it difficult in

---

Tips for Aerobic Exercise Class

• *Wear proper shoes. Jogging shoes are not good for aerobics since they don't provide lateral support. Look for a shoe that fits well, that flexes at the ball of the foot, and that has good arch support in the insole and a solid heel counter.*
• *Be sure your routine includes a warm-up and a cool-down with stretching. This will help prevent muscle pulls.*
• *Don't bounce while stretching.*
• *Wear loose-fitting clothing. Cotton is a good choice because it absorbs sweat.*
• *Be sure to check your pulse rate at least once during your workout. Work at your own pace.*
• *Don't overextend on kicks or when stretching. Do what feels best for you; don't compare yourself with anyone else.*
• *When landing during high-impact aerobics, land on the balls of your feet and roll back to your heels to absorb shock. Make sure your heels touch the ground.*
• *If you get stronger and want to wear wrist weights, start easily. Don't add too much weight too soon. Never use ankle weights while doing aerobic exercise routines.*

---

low-impact routines to get their heart rates up high enough to enjoy the full benefits of an aerobic workout. Whatever the type of aerobic routine, avoid quick, jerky movements. Do not exercise on unyielding floors, even if you're doing low-impact aerobics. Hardwood floors and spring or padded floors are best.

Rope Jumping

Rope jumping is an inexpensive and convenient exercise that makes a good rainy-day alternative to running or biking. All you need to get started is a piece of rope or clothesline long enough to reach from armpit to armpit when passed under both your feet.

Jumping rope can be a good aerobic exercise if you can get the motion down well enough to continue for 20 to 30 minutes at a time. Rope jumping also helps develop coordination, balance, and agility, and it builds strength in your legs and forearms.

Select a pace that's comfortable for you. Start at about 60 turns per minute, then build to 70 to 100 turns. Rest if you need to. Stop and take your pulse halfway through a 20- or 30-minute session. It might take a while to build the strength to be able to jump for long periods. Interval training (see page 21) is the best way to build up to 20 to 30 minutes of straight jumping. For example, you might jump for three minutes and rest for one. You can vary your time of jumping versus resting, your pace, or the number of sets you do.

To help prevent shinsplints, ankle injury, and stress fractures, you should add a selection of the strengthening and stretching exercises described in the ''Shinsplints and Ankle Sprains'' section of chapter 8 to your warm-up and cool-down; to help prevent back strain, add a selection of exercises from the ''Lower-Back Pain'' section.

When you become stronger, you can increase the intensity of your workout by jumping faster or for a longer time, or by using a weighted rope. Heavy ropes usually weigh from one to six pounds.

Rope jumping can be very jarring to your back. If you have lower-back problems or if jumping hurts your knees, do not jump rope; find another exercise.

Rope-Jumping Tips

• *Wear supportive shoes.*
• *Jump on a firm but resilient surface, such as a hardwood floor. Avoid jumping rope on unyielding surfaces.*
• *Stretch thoroughly before and after jumping rope. Pay special attention to stretches for the lower back, lower legs, and hamstrings.*
• *To alleviate boredom, watch television or listen to music.*
• *Build some variety into your routine by alternating between jumping on one foot and then the other, by crossing the rope, or by changing the direction from front-swing to back-swing.*
• *If you have trouble coordinating the jumping at first, try twirling the rope in one hand and jumping when the rope slaps the ground.*

Weight Training

Weight training is the most effective way to develop muscular strength and endurance, whether you use a weight machine, free weights, or calisthenic movements. If you follow through for the full range of motion, weightlifting can also increase flexibility.

If you want to build muscular strength, start with the heaviest weight you can lift for six to eight repetitions—but no more. Once you can do eight repetitions, add more weight and go back to six repetitions. To build muscular endurance, follow the same system of overloading, but start with a lighter weight and lift it for 15 to 25 repetitions. To build both strength and endurance, lift a moderate weight for 8 to 15 repetitions. You won't gain strength as fast as with a strength routine, but this strength *and* endurance routine is best for most people. Once you have achieved your desired level of strength and endurance, you can maintain it by continuing to do the same number of repetitions at the same weight.

If you want to build muscle bulk as well as strength, do as many repetitions as you can, rest for a few minutes, then do another set of the same exercise. Repeat the exercise for two or three sets.

Weight training may or may not enhance aerobic fitness; it all depends on how you structure your workout. If you want to use weight training as the aerobic portion of your workout, consider interval circuit training or calisthenic circuit training.

Interval Circuit Training In *interval circuit training*, you do a series of exercises one after another. You attempt to go through the circuit of about ten weight machines or free-weight stations at a prescribed pace. You should do 8 to 12 repetitions at each station in from 30 seconds to two minutes. You rest 15 to 45 seconds between exercises, as you move to the next machine, or prepare for the next free-weight lift. It takes about 20 to 25 minutes to go through the entire workout.

Interval circuit training using a weight machine or free weights should only be undertaken under professional supervision from a qualified instructor who can design a program that fits your needs, and who can demonstrate the correct form for each exercise. In addition, except for hand weights, exercises done with free weights should only be undertaken with another person, or *spotter,* present. A spotter protects the person lifting weights from the serious injuries that a mishandled or dropped barbell can cause.

A typical circuit-training series includes about two miles of rowing on a rowing machine, followed by such exercises as leg extension, leg curl, leg press, bench press, shoulder press, and overhead or lateral pullover. This is followed by about a ten-minute ride on a stationary bike. The lifting routine continues with bicep curls, tricep curls, and working the abdominals, and ends with a thorough cool-down.

If interval circuit training interests you, see chapter 7 for further guidance on how to find good facilities and qualified trainers.

Calisthenic Circuit Training   You can also work on aerobic fitness by following a *calisthenic circuit training* program. Instead of lifting weights, your routine consists of a group of calisthenic exercises repeated several times. Calisthenics involve using gravity and your body weight for resistance. They require little or no equipment. With this program, you work against the clock. The goal is to complete all the exercises as efficiently as possible, doing them with good form. As you become more fit, your time will improve.

The amount of work you do is based on your maximum effort per exercise. For example, if you can do 16 push-ups in one minute—your best effort—you should design your program around doing eight push-ups in 30 seconds. Doing a series of exercises at your maximum effort for three rounds (circuits) will overload your muscles and you'll improve.

Before you get started, you'll have to test yourself to determine the intensity of your work load. Test yourself on each exercise in the circuit to see how many times you can perform the exercises in one minute. Use half that amount as your starting level.

During the first week of your program, complete only one full circuit. During the second week, finish two full circuits. By the third week, you should be able to complete the entire circuit three times.

Your circuit should include about six or seven exercises for all your major muscle groups. Check your pulse rate after every circuit. If you're working too hard, slow down. Speed up if you're not working hard enough, but do not sacrifice good form for quantity.

For example, you could do a beginning calisthenic circuit as follows: jog in place for two minutes, then do push-ups (regular or modified),

---

Circuit-Training Tips

When doing either interval training with weights, under supervision, or calisthenic circuit training, keep these pointers in mind:
- *Breathe slowly and steadily. Never hold your breath.*
- *Exercise your largest muscle groups first. This stimulates blood circulation and helps prevent strain of secondary muscle groups. It's impossible to work your larger muscles to exhaustion if your smaller muscles give out first. The best order is lower back, buttocks, legs, chest, and abdominals.*
- *Focus on quality rather than quantity. Never sacrifice form or get sloppy just to do more repetitions.*
- *Perform each repetition slowly and steadily. Each lift should take about six seconds—two seconds to lift and four seconds to lower.*
- *Don't extend your joints beyond their normal range of motion (hyperextension).*
- *Whenever you're doing strength training with weights, always have a partner on hand as a spotter.*
- *When lifting weights on a bench, always keep your lower back pressed flat to the bench.*
- *Keep your neck muscles loose. Many people tense their necks when lifting weights, causing unnecessary tension and strain. Try doing the neck stretch described on page 44 when resting between stations or exercises.*
- *Make each motion slow and controlled. Jerky motion can cause muscle pulls.*
- *Since you're working your muscles to exhaustion, rest a day between workouts to give your body a chance to recover. If you want to work out every day, exercise the upper body one day and the lower body the next day.*

straight leg raises, scissors, side bends, and bent-knee sit-ups. Exercise at each station no longer than 30 seconds. An advanced circuit could include the following stations: rope jumping for three minutes, push-ups (chin-ups if a bar is available), straight leg raises *and* standing hip flexion, scissors *and* hydrants, side bends *and* trunk twists, and bent-knee sit-ups *and* bicycles. While doing advanced circuit intervals, perform each exercise no more than 30 seconds, for a maximum total of 60 seconds of exercise at each station. Do not undertake an advanced circuit until you're able to do so without strain.

Once you can do three circuits in 20 minutes, increase the number of repetitions for each exercise by one-fourth. If your work load is eight push-ups, increase it to ten.

Calisthenic circuit training can provide you with a change of pace when worked into your exercise schedule with other fitness activities such as jogging, walking, or bicycling.

Underwater Workouts

Most underwater workouts take advantage of the fact that it's much easier to stretch underwater and it's much more difficult to move around. You can design a stretching program to increase flexibility or work on muscle toning and cardiovascular conditioning through water aerobics workouts.

The support provided by the water makes underwater workouts very good for seniors and for the obese, as well as for people with joint problems or those recovering from an injury.

Some health clubs and "Y" organizations offer aerobic dance classes in the pool. You'll find it takes a lot of energy to perform even simple motions underwater. If you kick your leg on land, you provide the energy to kick it out, then gravity pulls it down. In water, you have to provide the energy to both raise and lower your leg.

You can also develop an aerobic workout designed around underwater running—wearing a flotation vest, you actually float as you move your legs in a running motion. Your feet never touch the ground, eliminating stress on impact, and the water provides resistance to your movement. Underwater running can be used to supplement your regular running routine, or to help in rehabilitation if you've been injured.

The following stretching exercises can be used to help you warm up for a swim or as a stretching routine. The second set of exercises can be used as part of an aerobic or strength-building routine.

When doing the stretches, stretch gradually, breathe regularly, and don't bounce or strain. Hold each stretch one time for 15 to 30 seconds. The same rules apply to an underwater workout as to a warm-up performed on dry land.

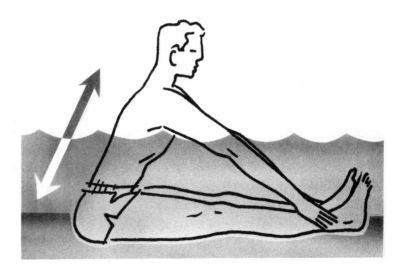

Sitting Hamstring Stretch

Sit on the bottom of the pool, in water up to your lower shoulders. Extend your legs straight out in front of you. Keep your toes pointed toward the ceiling and lean forward until you feel the stretch in your hamstrings, the muscles in the back of your thighs. Hold one time for 30 seconds.

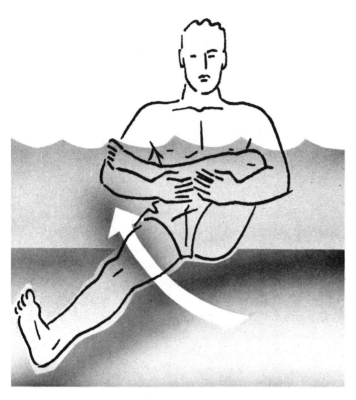

Buttocks Stretch

Sit on the bottom of the pool, in water up to your shoulders. Extend your right leg straight out in front of you and cross your left leg, placing your foot in your lap. Cradle your left ankle and knee, as shown, and gently pull your leg toward your chest. Hold one time for 30 seconds, and repeat with the opposite leg.

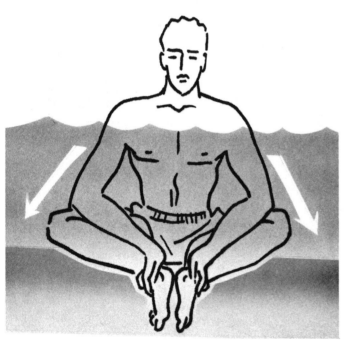

Sitting Groin Stretch

Sit on the bottom of the pool, in water up to your shoulders. Put the soles of your feet together and hold your ankles. Use your elbows to push down gently on your knees. Hold one time for 30 seconds.

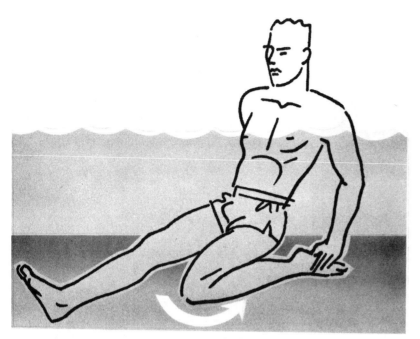

Sitting Quadricep Stretch

Sit on the bottom of the pool, in water up to your lower shoulders. Extend your right leg straight in front of you and bend your left leg behind you, as shown. Lean back slowly until you feel a stretch across your quadricep. Hold one time for 30 seconds, and repeat with the opposite leg.

Shoulder Stretch

Stand in the pool, in water up to your shoulders, with your back about two feet from the edge of the pool. Relax your shoulders and reach your arms behind your back. Grasp the edge of the pool. You should feel the stretch in your arms, chest, and shoulders. Hold one time for 30 seconds.

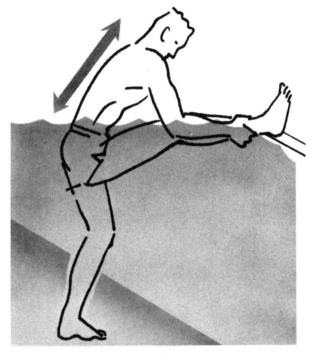

Standing Hamstring Stretch

Stand in the pool, in water up to your waist. Place your right leg straight in front of you, with your toes on the edge of the pool. Keep your left knee bent slightly and your right leg submerged. Bend from the hips and reach toward the toes of your right leg. Don't strain. Hold one time for 30 seconds, and repeat with the opposite leg.

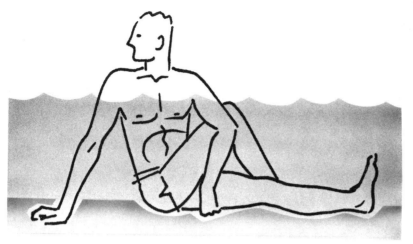

Trunk Twist

Sit on the bottom on the pool, in water up to your shoulders. Cross your legs as depicted. Turn at the hips to look behind you. Keep your back straight and your toes pointed toward the ceiling. Hold one time for 30 seconds, and repeat with the opposite leg.

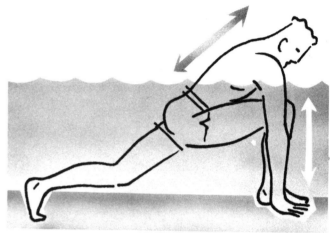

Runner's Stretch

Stand in the pool, in water up to your waist. Assume the racer's starting position and stretch your left leg backward as depicted. Keep your right knee perpendicular to your right ankle; do not extend your right knee beyond the ankle. Hold one time for 30 seconds, and repeat with the opposite leg.

Standing Quadricep Stretch

Stand in the pool, in water up to your shoulders. Bend your right leg at the knee. Hold your right foot behind your back and gently pull until you feel a stretch in your quadriceps. Hold one time for 30 seconds, and repeat with the opposite leg.

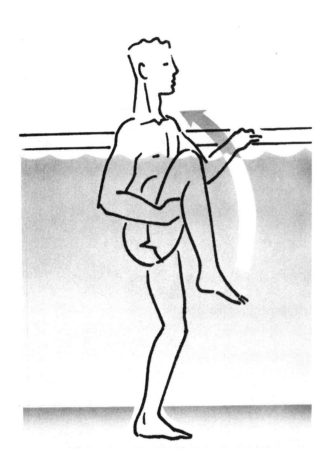

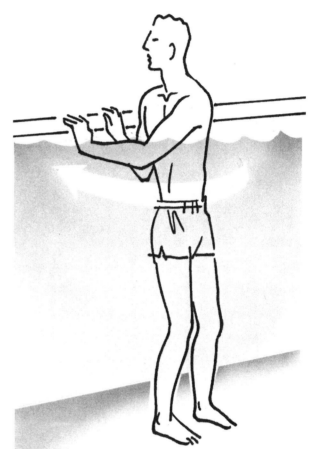

Knee Pull

Stand in the pool, in water up to your shoulders. Grip your right leg behind your knee and gently pull toward your chest. Hold one time for 30 seconds, and repeat with the opposite leg.

Standing Torso Twist

Stand in the pool, in water up to your shoulders. With your back to the edge of the pool, twist to the right and place the palms of your hands against the wall. Keep your back straight and your hips pointed forward. Hold one time for 30 seconds, then repeat in the opposite direction.

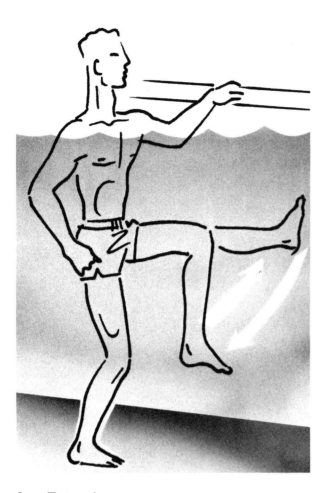

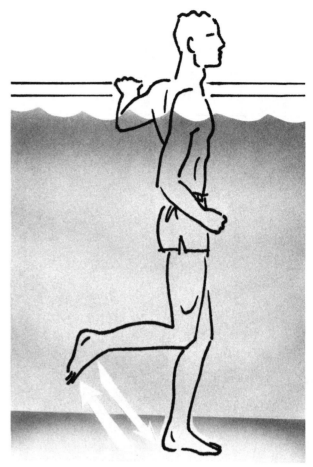

Leg Extension

Stand in the pool, in water up to your shoulders, with your knees bent slightly. Lift your left knee to form a 90-degree angle and extend your leg straight out in front of you. Do 10 repetitions, and repeat with the opposite leg. Gradually build to 20 repetitions with each leg.

Leg Curl

Stand in the pool, in water up to your shoulders. Hold the side of the pool for additional support. Lift your right leg at the knee to a 90-degree angle, then lower it to the bottom. Keep your back straight. Do 10 repetitions, then repeat with the opposite leg. Gradually build to 20 repetitions with each leg.

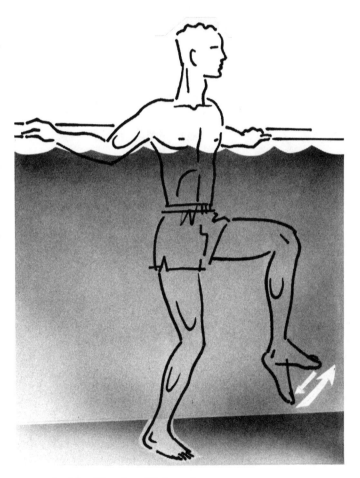

Ankle Flexion/Extension

Stand in the pool, in water up to your shoulders. Hold your left leg at a 90-degree angle in front of you. Alternately flex and point your foot. Do 10 repetitions, then repeat with the opposite foot. Gradually build to 20 repetitions with each foot.

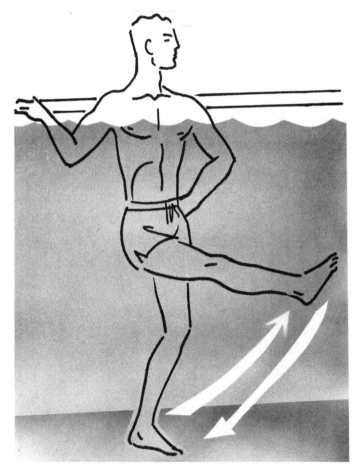

Hip Extension/Flexion

Stand in the pool, in water up to your shoulders. Kick your right leg out straight in front of you, then lower the leg. Do 10 repetitions, then repeat with the opposite leg. Gradually build to 20 repetitions with each leg. Repeat the same exercise, but kick your leg back behind you.

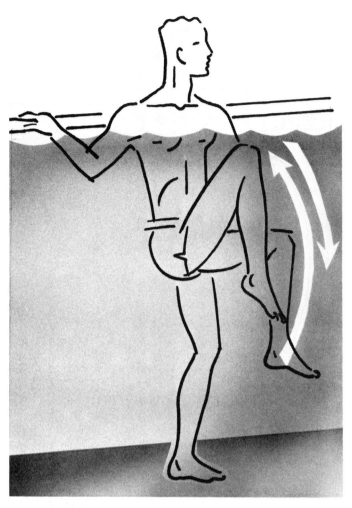

Modified Hip Flexion

(For people with lower-back problems.)

Stand in the pool, in water up to your shoulders. Bend your right knee at a 90-degree angle and raise your knee up toward your chest. Do 10 repetitions, then repeat with the opposite leg. Gradually build to 20 repetitions with each leg.

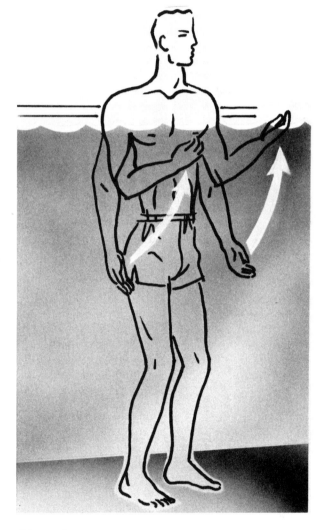

Bicep Curl

Stand in the pool, in water up to your shoulders. With your elbows at your sides, cup your hands with the palms facing away from you. Flex your elbows, curling your palms toward your chest. Do 10 repetitions. Gradually build to 20 repetitions with each arm.

Tricep Extension

Stand in the pool, in water up to your shoulders, with your knees bent slightly. Put your left hand on the side of the pool and swing your right arm from your side straight back behind you, then lower the arm. Do 10 repetitions, then repeat with the opposite arm. Gradually build to 20 repetitions with each arm.

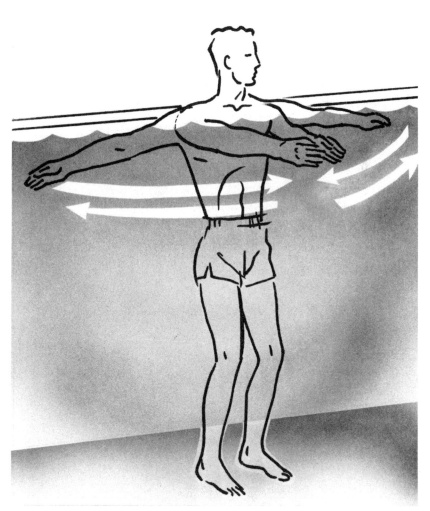

Chest Fly

Stand in the pool, in water up to your chest, with your knees bent slightly. Extend your arms straight out at your sides, then swing them straight out in front of you and return. Do 10 repetitions. Gradually build to 20 repetitions.

Stretching-Band Routines

Stretching bands are like giant rubber bands. They're used to provide resistance during exercise. Stretching-band routines do not improve aerobic fitness, but they can help develop muscle strength and flexibility. A stretching-band workout can supplement your regular aerobic program, for example.

Stretching bands are especially good for the elderly or for injury rehabilitation, because the user controls how much work is done, without the risk of dropping a dumbbell or a weight stack. They do have a drawback, in that you can't measure how much work you do, so on some days you might be tempted not to work as hard as you should.

You can work out with special stretching bands designed for exercise, or you can make your own bands from a bicycle inner tube, surgical tubing, or any other slightly elastic band. Select a tube of a thickness that matches your strength. Commercial stretching bands available in stores are usually color-coded according to resistance. If you make your own bands, you can increase resistance by doubling the thickness of the tube.

There are no limits to the kinds of exercises you can do using stretching bands. The following suggestions can help you get started. As with other exercise programs, you should warm up first, and cool down afterwards. For most exercises, you should hold the pull one time for 5 to 10 seconds. As you get stronger, you can increase the number of repetitions by intervals of five, up to 20 repetitions per exercise. You can also increase the number of sets—for example, going through the routine two or three times.

Bicep Curl

Sit in a chair and lean forward, with your back straight, your elbows on your knees, and both feet on the floor. Hook a band securely under your right foot. Slip the palm of your right hand under the other end of the band. With your elbow resting on your knee, flex your arm and pull toward your chest. Use your opposite forearm to brace your right elbow, as shown. Hold one time, 5 to 10 seconds, then repeat with the opposite arm.

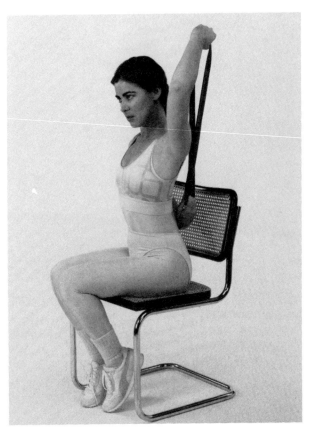

Tricep Curl

Sit in a chair with your back straight and both feet flat on the floor. Put your right hand behind your back and stretch your left arm up over your head as if you were scratching your shoulder blade. Hold one end of the band in each hand and pull. Hold one time for 5 to 10 seconds, then repeat, switching arm positions.

Chest Pull

Stand tall with your back straight and your knees bent slightly. Hold a small band with both hands at chest height in front of you. Keep your elbows bent. Pull your hands apart until you feel the band resist. Hold one time 5 to 10 seconds.

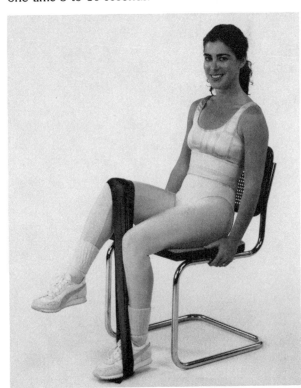

Hip Flexion

Sit in a chair, with your back straight and both feet flat on the floor. Hook one end of a band securely across the bottom of your left foot and hook the other end over your right knee. Lift your right leg off the ground until you feel the band resist. Keep your back straight. Hold one time for 5 to 10 seconds, and repeat with the opposite leg.

Outer-Thigh Push

Sit on the floor, with your legs extended straight in front of you. Hook a band around your calves, lean back, and support your upper body with your arms, as shown. Keep your back straight. Spread your legs until you feel the band resist. Hold one time for 5 to 10 seconds.

Inner-Thigh Pull

Sit on the floor, with your right leg bent at about a 45-degree angle and your left leg straight out in front of you. Hook one end of a band securely under the sole of your right foot and the other end across the middle of your left calf. Rotate your upper body toward your straight leg and support your body on your left arm, as shown. Keep your back comfortably straight and your right arm across your pelvis for support. Plant your right foot firmly and raise your left leg high enough to feel the band resist. Keep your left foot flexed and don't rotate at the ankle. Hold one time for 5 to 10 seconds. Repeat with the opposite leg.

Plyometrics

A plyometric drill is a series of explosive movements done with maximum energy, to increase muscle strength and speed. Plyometrics are very sport-specific. They can help you increase the power of your tennis serve, jump up to shoot a basket, improve your cross-country or downhill skiing and the like, but they are not used as part of a regular fitness program. The drills promote changes in the neuromuscular system that can help muscles respond more quickly to changes in direction. Plyometrics are *not* designed for beginners. You should be in excellent condition or you run the risk of pulling a muscle, twisting an ankle, or worse.

Most plyometric exercises involve a series of vertical jumps, hops, and leaps in which you coil your body down and inward, spring forward and up, uncoiling, then land and recoil. The power with which you can perform plyometrics depends upon the strength of the core of your body, the lower abdominal area. The impulse for a movement begins in the core and extends toward the peripheries—the arms and hands, legs and feet. The stronger your core muscles, the more power can be generated to the body peripheries.

Proper form is *essential;* stop exercising when you no longer have the strength to do the drill correctly. It's a good idea to have someone watch you do the drills. Your partner can watch for sloppy form, a sign that you're getting too tired.

Many of these drills might not appear taxing, but the key to plyometrics is to give each jump, hop, or twist your all. Maximum effort is required for best results. You'll be surprised at how strenuous it is to give maximum effort, using correct form, for ten or twelve consecutive repetitions.

The force and energy required make warm-up and stretching absolutely necessary before doing any plyometric drills. Generally, you should repeat two to three sets of eight to ten repetitions of a drill, with a one- or two-minute rest between sets. If you always give it your all, you will continually overload your muscles as you get stronger. Take a day off between workouts.

For fastest improvement, do plyometric drills two or three times a week. Plyometric drills don't improve your cardiovascular fitness, so they should

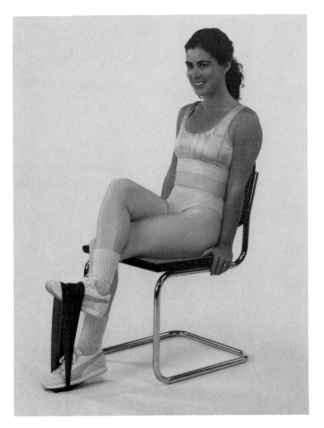

Ankle Flex

Sit in a chair, with your back straight and your right leg crossed over your left. Hook one end of a small band securely under your left foot and the other end across the arch of your right foot. Flex your right foot, and hold one time for 5 to 10 seconds. Repeat with the opposite leg.

supplement your regular aerobic workout routine. For example, if you want to build strength in your skiing, in addition to your regular conditioning you could try the downhill skiing drill shown on page 41. By putting out maximum effort and repeating the motion ten or twelve times in a row, you work the muscles and slowly teach them to respond to, for example, moguls or unweighting your skis. The following sample drills can give you an idea of how you can get started for other sports as well.

Basketball Drill

This drill helps build explosive leg strength that assists in basketball, and other sports involving jumping.
Start with your knees bent in a half squat and your arms held at your sides. Jump up and forward, swinging your arms forward to build height. Jump as far and as high as you can. Bend your knees to absorb the shock of landing. Resume the starting position. Do 10 jumps in a row, rest 2 minutes, then repeat. Do 3 to 5 sets of 10 jumps.

Downhill Skiing Drill

This drill is helpful in developing ankle strength and balance that can be helpful in downhill skiing, tennis, and football.

Stand with your knees bent slightly, and hop from side to side. Bend your knees to absorb the shock of landing. Hold your arms out at your sides to help you keep your balance. Jump back and forth as high and as far as you can, 10 times in each direction. Rest for 1 minute. Repeat 5 sets of 10 jumps.

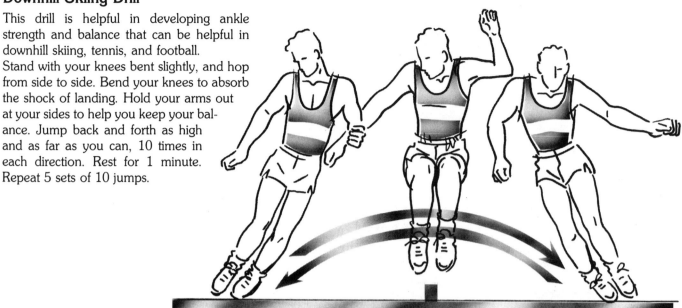

Running Drill

This drill helps develop striding power for running or cross-country skiing.

Stand with one leg extended and flexed at a right angle in front of you, the other leg extended behind you as if you had taken a long step. Jump up as high as you can, swinging your arms to build height. Switch the positions of your legs in midair, then land with the opposite leg in front. Bend your front knee to absorb the impact of landing. Do 10 jumps, 5 with each leg extended. Rest for 1 or 2 minutes, then repeat. Do 3 sets of 10 jumps.

Swimming Drill

This exercise helps build trunk strength that is helpful in swimming, baseball, cross-country skiing, and most sports that involve throwing.

Stand with your feet shoulder-width apart and your knees bent slightly. Place a weighted bar with 20 to 30 pounds on it across your shoulders and hold it firmly, with your arms fully extended. Twist your upper body to the left. Halfway through the twist, use the muscles in your torso to overcome the momentum and reverse direction. Before your torso is rotated fully, reverse direction and swing in the opposite direction. Repeat 10 to 20 times in each direction. Rest 1 minute, then repeat. Do 3 to 5 sets.

Tennis Drill

This exercise helps build agility and power to train the muscles for fast changes in direction. It is good for developing the explosive first step in tennis, basketball, and other sports involving changes in direction.

Place a stack of pillows on the ground and make a mark or set up a cone or flag as a finish line 15 yards in front of the pillows. Start the drill by jumping back and forth over the pillows six times, as fast as you can. Keep your feet together and make sure that both feet touch the ground. Be prepared on the last landing to sprint forward to the finish line. Do 6 jumps and a spring, then rest 1 minute. Do 3 to 5 sets.

5

Breaking a Sweat

Warm Up, Cool Down

Before you start your workout, it's very important to take about ten or fifteen minutes to *warm up*. During the warm-up, you first increase the blood circulation to your muscles, and you then stretch your muscles to prepare them for strenuous activity. Supple, well-stretched muscles don't directly benefit your heart or lungs, but they will make you much less susceptible to injury.

You should warm up slightly before stretching, because warmer muscles can be stretched more easily without risk of pulls or tears. Start by jogging in place, riding a stationary bicycle at a moderate pace, or doing some calisthenic exercises for two to three minutes. After you get your blood circulating and your muscles warm, stop and stretch.

You should do slow, static stretches, holding a muscle in a stretched-out position for 10 to 30 seconds. As you stretch a muscle, you'll feel a resistance like the tension in a rubber band. Stretch until you feel slight tension, but *never* to the point of pain. Don't bounce. Bouncing can cause muscle tears. Breathe slowly and steadily; inhale through your nose, exhale through your mouth.

You can become more flexible by stretching, but don't compare yourself with anyone else. Some people are born more flexible than others. Women tend to be more supple than men, and after age 30 both men and women tend to lose flexibility. After several weeks of consistent stretching, your muscle elasticity will increase and you'll be able to stretch further.

After your workout, always give your body a chance to recover slowly and *cool down*. If you exercise hard and then stop suddenly, your heart continues to pump hard, but your leg muscles no longer help to force the blood back to the heart. If this happens, your blood can "pool" in your lower extremities, leaving your internal organs and brain temporarily short of adequate blood supply. This can cause dizziness, fainting, or vomiting. The cool-down period also helps prevent the buildup of lactic acid, a chemical by-product of exercise. Lactic acid in the muscle leads to muscle soreness. The more you stretch during cool-down, the less likely you are to feel the effects of exercise the next day.

To cool down, continue the activity you've been doing, but at a slower pace, for two to three minutes. If you were jogging, slow down and walk for a few minutes. If you were cycling, pedal in a lower gear. To maintain flexibility, your cool-down should also include at least five minutes of additional stretching *after* you exercise. The following exercises can be used for both warm-up and cool-down stretching.

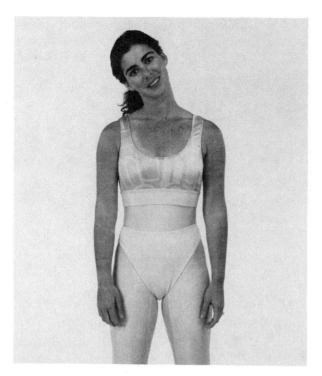

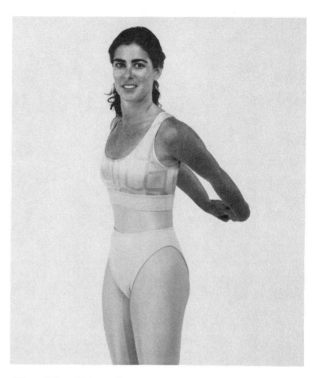

Neck Stretch

Stand tall with your back straight, and relax your shoulders. Tilt your head to the right, to the rear, to the left, and then forward. Hold each position 10 seconds, repeat 5 to 10 times in each direction. Do *not* roll your neck, but gently stretch it in each direction.

Shoulder Stretch

Stand tall, with your shoulders relaxed. Stretch your arms behind your back and clasp your hands. Lift your arms behind you until you feel a stretch in your arms, chest, and shoulders. Keep your shoulders down and as relaxed as possible. Hold one time for 30 seconds.

Tricep Stretch

Reach your left arm overhead and extend your arm behind you as if to scratch your shoulder blade. Place your right hand on your left elbow and gently pull behind you to extend the stretch. Hold one time for 30 seconds. Repeat with your arms switched.

Groin Stretch

Sit on the floor, with the soles of your feet pressed together. Hold your ankles and gently press your knees down with your elbows. Keep your back straight. Remember to breathe slowly and steadily. *Don't bounce.* Hold one time for 30 seconds.

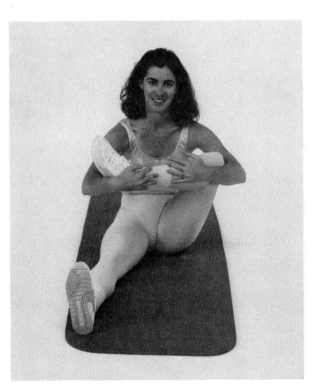

Buttocks Stretch

Sit on the floor, with your right leg straight in front of you and your left leg crossed in your lap. Cradle your left ankle and knee in your arms, as shown, and gently pull your leg toward your chest. Keep your back straight and your right leg flat on the floor, toes pointed toward the ceiling. Hold one time for 30 seconds. Repeat with the opposite leg.

Hamstring Stretch

Sit on the floor with your left leg straight out in front of you and your right leg tucked against your right thigh, close to the body. Reach for the ankle of the extended leg. Flex from the hips and keep your back straight. *Don't bounce.* You should feel a gentle stretch along your hamstrings, the muscles in the back of your thigh. Hold one time for 30 seconds, then repeat with the opposite leg.

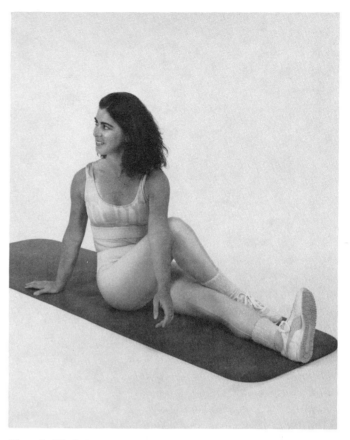

Modified Hamstring Stretch

Stand with your left leg resting on the back of a chair or on a counter. Keep your right leg slightly bent. Reach for the ankle of the extended leg. Flex from the hips and keep your back straight. *Don't bounce.* You should feel a gentle stretch along your hamstrings, the muscles in the back of your thigh. Hold one time for 30 seconds, then repeat with the opposite leg.

Trunk Twist

Sit on the floor, with your legs crossed as shown. Rotate at the hips and look behind you. Keep your back straight and the toes of the extended foot pointed toward the ceiling. Hold one time for 30 seconds. Switch leg positions and repeat.

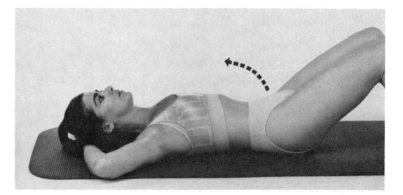

Pelvis Tilt

Lie on your back on the floor, with your legs bent and your feet flat on the floor. Squeeze your buttocks together and rotate your pelvis upward. Your lower back will press to the floor. Hold the tilt for 3 to 5 seconds. Repeat 10 times.

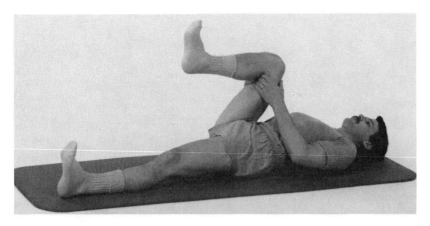

Single Leg Pull

Lie on your back on the floor, with one knee bent and the other leg flat on the floor. Flex both your feet. Grip your right leg just behind the knee and gently pull toward your chest. Hold one time for 30 seconds. Repeat with the opposite leg.

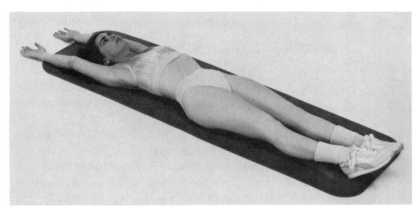

Full-Body Stretch

Lie flat on your back on the floor, with your arms extended over your head. Stretch your arms and legs, lengthening your arms, shoulders, ribcage, abdominals, spine, legs, and feet. Breathe slowly and steadily. Hold one time for 30 seconds.

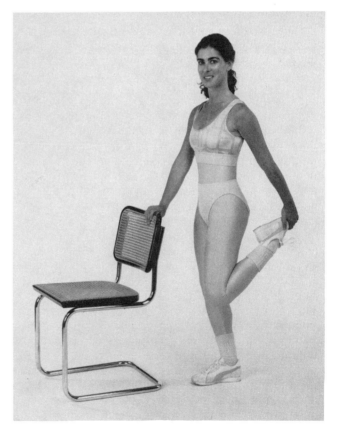

Quadriceps Stretch

Stand with your back straight and your knees slightly bent. Hold a chairback or counter to keep your balance as you bend your left leg behind you, and grasp the foot with your left hand. Gently pull your foot upward until you feel a stretch across your quadricep, the muscle along the front of your thigh. Hold one time for 30 seconds. Repeat with the opposite leg.

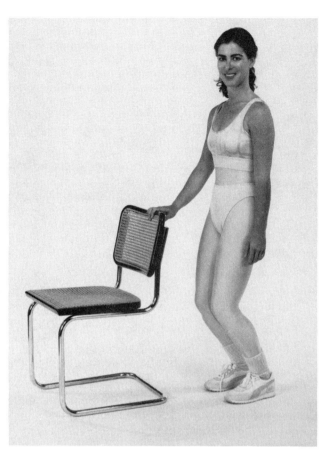

Modified Quadriceps Stretch

(For older individuals or people with back problems. *Note:* This is not actually a stretch, but a mild eccentric contraction, or lengthening of the muscle fibers. It warms up the muscle and may improve flexibility.)

Stand tall and hold a chairback or counter to help you keep your balance. Slowly bend your knees. Keep your back straight and your weight over your pelvis. You should feel your quadriceps working—the muscles along the fronts of your thighs. Hold one time for 30 seconds.

Calf Stretch

Stand about two feet from a wall. Bend your left knee and stretch your right leg behind you. Keep your left leg straight, with your foot flat on the floor and your toes pointed straight ahead. Keep your back straight and aligned with the extended leg. Lean forward to feel a stretch along your calf muscle. Hold one time for 30 seconds. Repeat with the opposite leg.

To isolate and stretch your ankle, keep your heel flat on the floor and slightly flex your back knee. Hold one time for 30 seconds, and repeat with the opposite leg.

Strengthening Exercises

Spot reducing doesn't work. Even doing 100 sit-ups a night won't eliminate a roll of fat around your abdomen. The only way to get rid of unwanted pounds is to diet and do aerobic exercise. If you stick to your exercise routine, you'll lose your stomach bulge and the fat from the rest of your body.

That's not to say those 100 sit-ups won't do you any good. They will strengthen the abdominal muscles that lie beneath the fat. The following exercises can help you strengthen the muscles in your chest, arms, abdomen, thighs, hips, and buttocks.

When exercising, be sure to breathe slowly and deeply. During most exercises, it's best to exhale on *exertion* and inhale on release; breathe out when lifting, and in when lowering the weight. This method is preferable because people have a tendency not to take a full breath if they inhale during exertion.

CHEST AND ARMS

Reverse Dips

Hold the sides of a chair, with your legs extended in front of you, as shown. Bend your arms as though you were going to sit on the floor in front of the chair. Alternately straighten and bend your arms, lifting and lowering your body. Do not lock your elbows. Repeat 10 times, and gradually build to 20 repetitions.

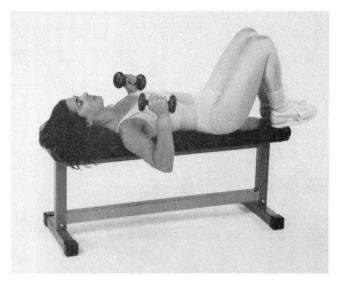

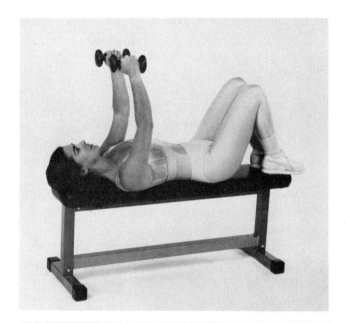

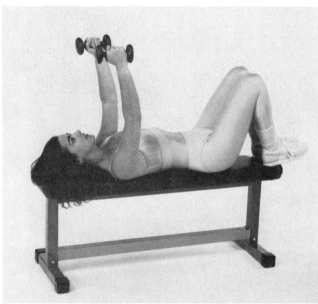

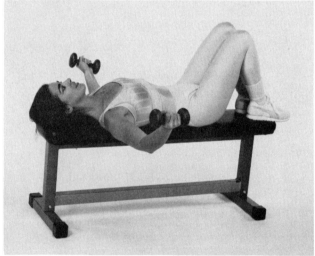

Bench Press

Lie on your back on a bench, with your knees bent and your feet resting on the end of the bench. Hold a 5-to-10-pound hand weight in each hand, just above your chest. Slowly press them above you until your arms are straight, but don't lock your elbows. Lower and repeat 10 times, and gradually build to 20 repetitions. When you can do 20 repetitions easily, increase the hand weights to 10 to 20 pounds and start again at 10 repetitions.

Lateral Raise

Lie on your back on a bench, with your knees bent and your feet resting on the end of the bench. Raise a pair of 1-to-3-pound hand weights above your chest. Bend your arms and drop your elbows straight out at your sides. Don't let your elbows fall below bench level. Keep your lower back flat on the bench and your wrists curled. Don't lock your elbows. Return to the starting position. Repeat 10 times, and gradually build to 20 repetitions. When you can do 20 repetitions easily, increase the hand weights to 3 to 5 pounds and start again at 10 repetitions.

Regular Push-ups

Lie facedown on the floor, with your palms at your sides, fingers pointed forward and your ankles flexed, toes bent under. Keeping your back straight, push off the ground and raise your body until your arms are straight. *Don't lock your elbows.* Keep your head aligned with your spine. Lower your body, but do not rest on the ground. Repeat 10 times, and gradually build to 20 repetitions.

Push-ups from Knees

Lie facedown on the floor, with your palms at your sides, fingers pointed forward, and your legs bent, with toes pointed toward the ceiling. Keeping your back straight, push off the ground and raise your upper body from your knees until your arms are straight. *Don't lock your elbows.* Keep your head aligned with your spine. Lower your body, but do not rest on the ground. Repeat 10 times, and gradually build to 20 repetitions.

 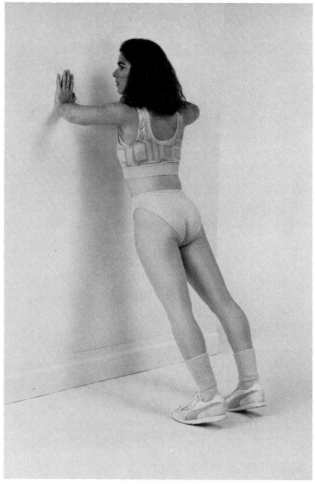

Push-ups Against a Wall

Lean into a wall at a 45-degree angle. Rest against the wall with your arms extended and your elbows slightly bent. Slowly bend your arms and lower your body until you touch the wall. Push back to starting position. Repeat 10 times, and gradually build to 20 repetitions.

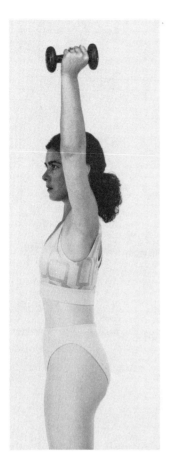 

Tricep Extension

Stand tall with your knees bent slightly, and hold a 1-to-3-pound hand weight above your head with one hand. Keep the raised elbow behind your ear, and slowly bend your arm at the elbow, lowering the weight behind your head. Don't arch your back. Repeat 10 times, and gradually build to 20 repetitions. Repeat with the opposite arm. When you can do 20 repetitions easily, increase the hand weights to 5 to 10 pounds and start again at 10 repetitions.

Bicep Curl

Stand tall, with your back straight and your knees bent slightly. Hold a 1-to-3-pound hand weight in each hand, with your palms facing up. Slowly flex your elbows and raise the weights. Repeat 10 times, and gradually build to 20 repetitions. When you can do 20 repetitions easily, increase the weights to 5 to 10 pounds and start again at 10 repetitions.

Overhead Press

Stand tall with your knees bent slightly. Hold a 1-to-3-pound hand weight in each hand at shoulder level. Keep your palms facing forward. Press the weights overhead, then lower to shoulder level. Repeat 10 times, and gradually build to 20 repetitions. When you can do 20 repetitions easily, increase the weights to 5 to 10 pounds and start again at 10 repetitions.

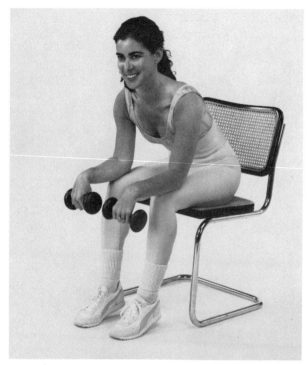

Wrist Curls

Sit in a chair, with your back straight and your forearms resting on your thighs. Grip a 1-to-3-pound weight in each hand with your palms facing up. Using your forearms, flex your wrists and curl the weights. Keep your elbows and forearms down. Repeat 10 to 12 times.

Reverse Wrist Curl

Sit in a chair, with your back straight and your forearms resting on your thighs. Grip a 1-to-3-pound weight in each hand with your palms facing down. Using your forearms, extend your wrists and curl the weights. Keep your elbows and forearms down. Repeat 10 to 12 times.

ABDOMINALS

Side Bends

Stand tall with your knees bent slightly, your feet shoulder-width apart, and your hands behind your head. Bend to one side until you feel the stretch, then bend to the other side. Repeat 10 times in each direction, and gradually build to 20 repetitions.

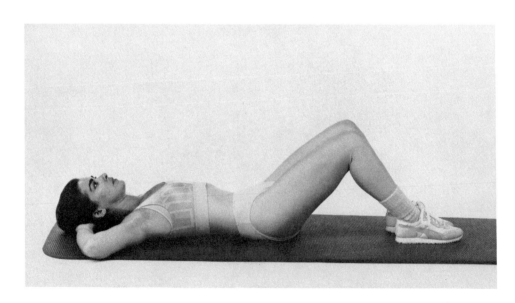

Bicycles

Lie on your back on the floor, with your knees up and your toes pointed, as shown. Roll your shoulder blades off the floor, then alternate touching your right elbow to your left knee and your left elbow to your right knee. Don't pull on your head or neck. Keep your lower back pressed against the floor. Repeat 10 times on each side, then gradually build to 20 repetitions.

Bent-Knee Sit-ups

Lie on your back on the floor, with your knees bent and your feet flat on the floor. Interlace your fingers loosely behind your neck for support. Roll up until your shoulder blades are off the floor. Keep your abdominals tight and your lower back pressed to the floor. Breathe out on the contraction, and don't pull on your head or neck. Repeat 10 times, and gradually build to 20 repetitions.

Stomach Crunches

Lie on your back on the floor, your fingers loosely interlaced behind your head. Bring your knees up and point your toes. Roll your shoulder blades up and keep them off the floor. Keep your lower back pressed to the floor. Use your abdominals to touch your knees with your elbows. Repeat 10 times, and gradually build to 20 repetitions.

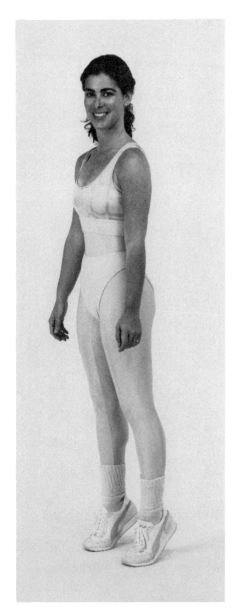

Straight Leg Raises

Lie on your back on the floor, with your left leg bent and your left foot flat on the floor. Extend your right leg straight out in front of you. Keep your right foot flexed and your lower back flat on the floor. Slowly raise and lower your right leg 10 to 12 times. Repeat with the opposite leg. Add 1-pound ankle weights when your legs and abdomen become stronger.

Calf Raises

Stand with your back straight, with your knees bent slightly, and your feet pointing straight ahead of you. Raise up on the balls of your feet, then lower yourself down. Keep the motion smooth and controlled; *don't bounce.* Repeat 10 times, and gradually build to 20 repetitions.

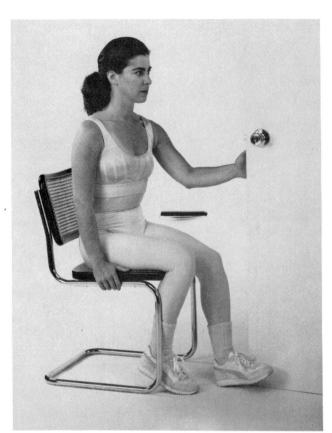

Ankle Push

Sit in a chair in front of an open door. Place the outside of your left foot against the edge of the door. Hold the door and push your foot against the door. Hold for 7 seconds. Do 5 repetitions with your left foot, then repeat the exercise with the opposite foot. Gradually build to 10 repetitions with each foot.

Ankle Rotation

Sit in a chair with your right leg crossed over your left. Rotate your foot at the ankle back and forth, 10 times in each direction. Repeat with the opposite ankle. Gradually build to 20 rotations in each direction.

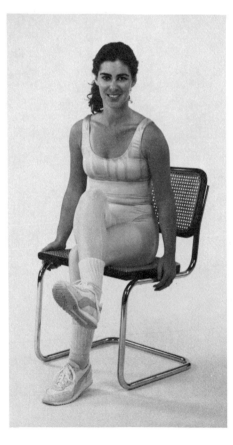

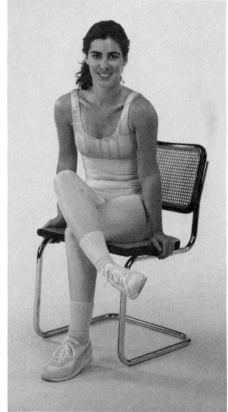

Half Squats

Stand with your back straight and your knees bent slightly. Bend your knees to about a quarter squat position. Return to the standing position. Repeat 10 times, and gradually build to 20 repetitions.

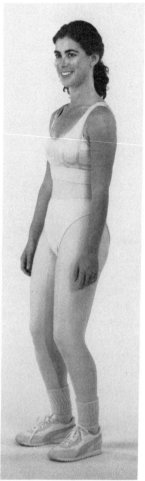

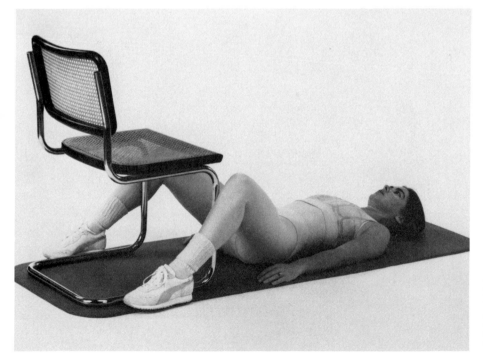

Thigh Squeeze

Lie on your back on the floor, with your knees bent and your feet flat on the floor. Place a chair inside your inner thighs and squeeze your knees together. Hold for 10 seconds, then relax. Repeat 5 times. Keep your lower back pressed to the floor.

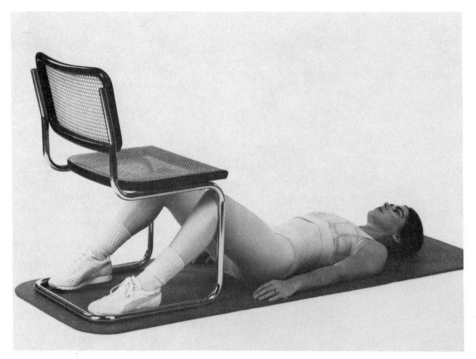

Thigh Push

Lie on your back on the floor, with your knees bent and your feet flat on the floor. Slide underneath a sturdy chair and place your thighs between the legs of the chair. Spread your legs, pushing against the legs of the chair. Push for 10 seconds, then relax. Repeat 5 times.

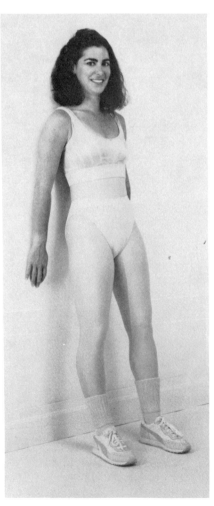 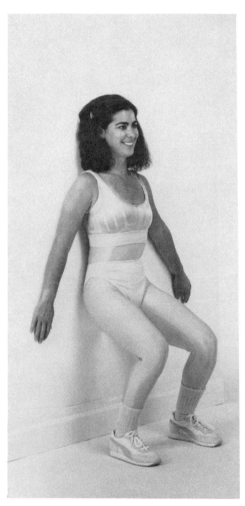

Half Squat Against a Wall

Lean with your back flat against a wall, your heels about one foot from the baseboard, and your arms at your sides. Bend your knees to about a quarter squat position. Return to standing position. Repeat 10 times. Gradually build to 20 repetitions.

One-Legged Squat with Chair

Stand about one foot in front of a sturdy chair. Bend at the hips and grip the sides of the chair seat. Lift your left leg and slowly bend your right leg to a quarter squat position, then straighten. Do 10 repetitions, and repeat with the opposite leg. Gradually build to 20 repetitions with each leg.

HIPS AND BUTTOCKS

Chair Step-ups

Stand in front of a sturdy chair. Step up, then step down. Alternate legs. When stepping down, be sure your toes touch the ground first. Repeat 10 times with each foot, and gradually build to 20 repetitions.

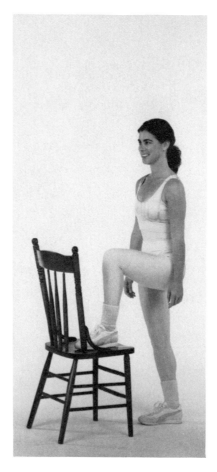 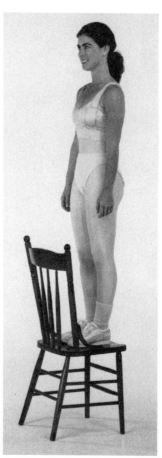

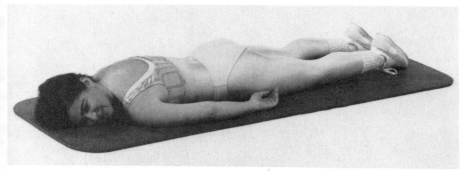

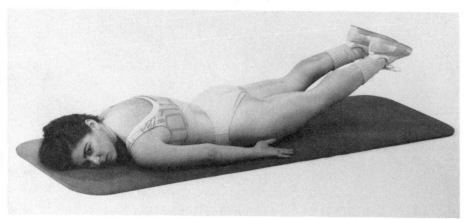

Reverse Leg Raises

Don't do this exercise if you have lower-back problems. Lie face-down on the floor, with your head resting at one side and your arms down at each side. Squeeze your buttocks together and lift both legs off the floor. Repeat 10 times. Gradually build to 20 repetitions.

Kick Back

Don't do this exercise if you have lower-back problems. Kneel on the floor and slowly raise your left knee in toward your chest, then extend it above and behind your back. Don't arch your back. Straighten your leg and hold for one second, then return the knee to the chest. Do 10 repetitions, and repeat with the opposite leg. Gradually build to 20 repetitions.

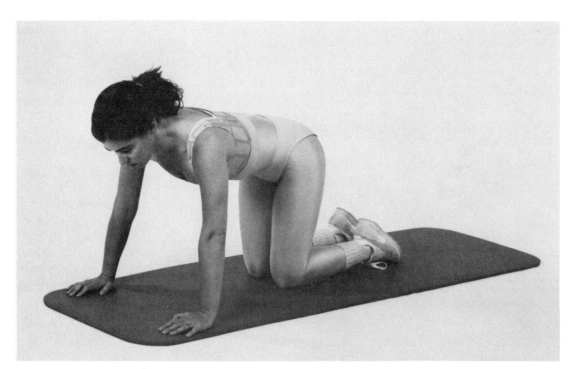

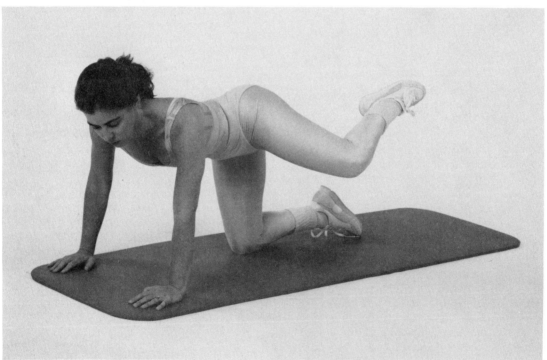

Hydrants

Kneel on the floor. Keep your leg bent, and raise your left leg to the side toward the ceiling. Keep your hips parallel to the floor and don't arch your back. Lower the leg and do 10 repetitions, then repeat with the opposite leg. Gradually build to 20 repetitions.

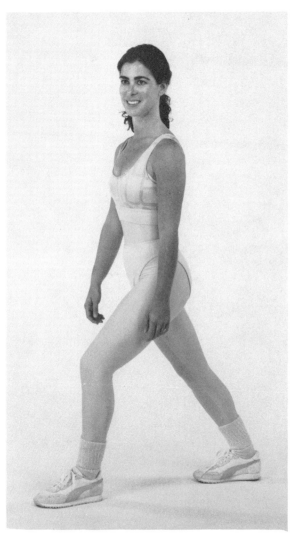 

Lunges

Stand with your left foot about two feet in front of your right foot. Keep your right leg straight and slowly bend your left knee. Let the right heel lift from the floor. *Don't* let your left knee move in front of the ankle or you will put unnecessary strain on your knee. Do 10 repetitions, and repeat with legs switched. Gradually build to 20 repetitions with each leg.

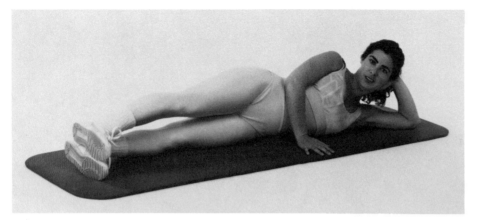

Side Leg Raises

Lie on the floor on your left side. Support your head with the palm of your hand, as shown. Keep your right leg straight, your ankles flexed, and your hips slightly forward. Raise your upper right leg, as shown, then lower it to starting position. Do 10 repetitions, then repeat on the opposite side. Gradually build to 20 repetitions on each side. When your legs become stronger, add 1-pound ankle weights.

Back Hyperextension

(*Note:* More than a strengthening exercise, the Back Hyperextension is recommended as an adjunct stretching exercise to the other exercises in this section.)

Lie on your stomach on the floor, with your legs straight and flat on the floor. Use your arms to push your upper body off the floor, keeping your hips pressed to the floor. Keep your elbows slightly bent; don't strain. Hold for 30 seconds, then lower. Repeat three times.

Standing Hip Flexion

Stand tall with your knees bent slightly. Raise your left knee toward your chest. Push down with your left hand for 10 seconds. Switch hands. While pushing down with your right hand, rotate your hip inward, as shown. Hold and continue to push down for 10 seconds, then push down with your left hand again and rotate the hip outward, as shown. Hold and continue to push down for 10 seconds, then return to the forward position. Do 10 repetitions, and repeat with the opposite leg. Gradually build to 20 repetitions for each leg.

Training Tips

When you're working out on your own, you're bound to have questions you'd like to ask a trainer or coach. The tips listed below answer many frequently asked questions.

• **When to exercise.** It doesn't matter what time of day you exercise. You are more likely to exercise at a time when your energy level is high, which is why "morning people" tend to prefer 6:00 A.M. workouts and "nighttime people" usually wait until after work. If you're training for a particular athletic event, for example a 10-kilometer race that starts at 8:00 A.M., you should prepare yourself by adjusting your training time to the mornings several weeks before the event.

• **Exercise and metabolism.** Exercise increases your metabolic rate both during and after exercise. The body burns calories at a faster rate four to twelve hours after exercise. If you're just getting started in an exercise program, your metabolism will stay elevated longer than it will when you're in better physical condition.

• **Exercise and smoking.** Smoking limits the amount of air your lungs can take in. Your cardiovascular system has to work harder to supply the oxygen needed during exercise. The more you smoke, the harder your heart has to work.

• **Exercise after eating.** If you eat two to three hours before exercise, you have time to digest your food, but not enough time to feel hungry again. Choose foods high in carbohydrates, and avoid fatty, spicy, and salty foods. It's safe to exercise on an empty stomach, but most people prefer eating something light before exercise.

• **How to breathe during exercise.** Breathe rhythmically through your mouth and nose at whatever pace is comfortable to you. Never hold your breath during exercise. Most experienced distance runners coordinate their breathing with their stride, inhaling for several strides, then exhaling for the same number of strides.

• **Drinking water during exercise.** It's essential that you drink plenty of water during prolonged exercise. Water helps prevent heat disorders and dehydration. During prolonged exercise in hot weather, you may sweat up to two liters of water per hour—the equivalent of five pounds of body weight.

If you exercise for 45 minutes or longer, you should take a break and drink small quantities of water. Drink more than you thirst for; you quench thirst long before you satisfy your body's need for fluids. Drink two eight-ounce glasses of water before exercising, and four to six ounces of water every 10 to 15 minutes during exercise. Replace the fluids gradually; the body cannot absorb more than eight to ten ounces of water every 20 minutes.

It's perfectly safe to drink cold water during and after exercising. Some people wrongly believe that drinking cold water causes stomach cramps or heart problems. Evidence indicates that cold water helps rehydrate the body because it can be absorbed more rapidly than warm water.

• **Mineral-replacement beverages.** There is no advantage to drinking mineral-replacement or special exercise beverages. When you exercise, your body needs water, and the body can absorb plain water faster than sugared drinks. (The major ingredients of most of the drinks are water and sugar, either glucose or sucrose.) Sugared drinks may actually increase your body's need for water. If you insist on using one of these drinks, dilute it with water.

• **The effects of heat and humidity.** Heat and humidity slow down your body's cooling system. The body cools itself through the evaporation of sweat. In hot, humid weather the air is already saturated with moisture and your sweat can't evaporate easily. Your body temperature stays high. If you dry your skin with a towel before your sweat can evaporate, you undermine your cooling system. To avoid overheating, exercise in the early morning or late afternoon or evening, when temperatures are lowest. In hot weather try swimming, which helps control your temperature during exercise.

• **Adjusting to hot-weather workouts.** It takes about four to ten days before your body can adjust to hot weather. In the heat, reduce the intensity of your workout initially, then slowly build back up to your normal workout. Ease up on hot days. Give yourself a chance to cool off at intervals during your workout. As you adjust to the heat, your body will begin to produce sweat with a lower concentration of salt.

• **Exercise and smog.** It's not safe to exercise outdoors if there's a smog alert or if the air quality is poor. People with asthma, angina, emphysema, or other cardiorespiratory problems should avoid outdoor exercise when the air quality is fair or poor. If you exercise outdoors in a smoggy area, do it in the early morning or late evening, when lighter traffic, cooler temperatures, and lower humidity improve the air quality. Go indoors if you develop eye irritation or respiratory discomfort.

• **Exercising when you feel sick.** Don't exercise if you have a fever. If your temperature is normal but you're feeling slightly under the weather, take your pulse. If your pulse is ten beats faster than your normal resting pulse rate, don't exercise. If your pulse rate is normal, go ahead and exercise, but reduce the intensity of your workout.

• **Cold-weather workouts.** If you're dressed properly and use good judgment, it's safe to work out during the winter, even in subfreezing temperatures. People with heart problems should not exercise outdoors in severe cold. When you exercise, you burn calories and raise the temperature of the blood circulating through the body. If you dress to keep heat from escaping, you'll be surprised how warm you'll get, even on the coldest days.

• **What to wear during cold-weather workouts.** The clothing you should wear during cold weather depends on air temperature, wind speed, humidity, and the intensity of your exercise. If you overdress, you'll sweat, and the chilling effect of your evaporating perspiration and cold, wet clothing may cause problems. Dress in layers. The first layer should be an evaporation layer of cotton or polypropylene material. Add an insulating layer to trap body heat, for example a layer of wool, which is a good insulator even when wet. Complete the cold-weather outfit with a windbreaker, a hat, and mittens or gloves.

• **What to wear during rain or snow.** Your body heat can't escape most waterproof clothing. Eventually, you'll find sweat trickling down inside your clothes. As in cold weather, rapid evaporation of sweat can result in loss of body heat and chills. To avoid this, choose ventilated rainwear that "breathes," such as that made of Gore-Tex or Klimate.

• **Breathing cold air.** You don't need to worry about breathing freezing air unless you have asthma. By the time the cold air reaches your lungs, it has been warmed. Cold, dry air may feel irritating to your throat, but you can avoid that by wrapping a scarf around your face.

• **Caffeine and exercise.** The caffeine in two cups of coffee taken one hour before exercising has been shown to delay the onset of exhaustion during endurance exercise because it helps in the metabolism of fat. Caffeine also elevates the heart rate and stimulates urine production, which might cause discomfort during a long-distance event.

• **Exercise at high altitudes.** Most people don't have any problems exercising at altitudes up to 6,500 feet. At higher altitudes, the oxygen content of the air is thinner, making your cardiorespiratory system work harder to circulate the same amount of oxygen. Avoid strenuous exercise until you adjust to the altitude, usually after two to five days.

• **Calories and the cold.** You will burn more calories exercising in the cold because your body's metabolic system has to work harder to keep warm.

• **Protein, vitamin, or mineral supplements.** You don't need to take any supplements if you stick to a balanced diet. Although potassium and iron may, in some cases, be depleted by prolonged vigorous exercise, you don't need expensive commercial supplements. Just eat plenty of vegetables, citrus fruits, and bananas for additional potassium, and meat, fish, beans, leafy green vegetables, and dried fruits for additional iron.

• **Carbohydrate loading.** Some long-distance runners try to build their energy reserves to the maximum level by carefully controlling what they eat before a race. About seven days before the event, they exercise very hard for 60 to 90 minutes, almost to the point of exhaustion. This depletes glycogen reserves, the carbohydrates stored in muscles for fuel. For the next three or four days they continue their regular training program, but severely restrict their carbohydrate intake (the source of glycogen), replacing carbohydrates with a high-fat and high-protein diet. Three or four days before competition, they then drastically increase their carbohydrate consumption by eating spaghetti, bread, potatoes, and other high-carbohydrate foods. In theory, carbohydrate loading results in high levels of glycogen in the muscles, which can be used during prolonged exercise. Carbohydrate loading doesn't help sprinters or athletes who exercise for less than 90 minutes at a time. Normal glycogen reserves are sufficient for that amount of work.

• **Hitting the wall.** The expression "hitting the wall" refers to a condition that occurs when the body has used up most of its energy stores because it has depleted its glycogen reserves. Athletes "hit the wall" after two to two and a half hours of aerobic exercise.

• **Steroids.** Some athletes take anabolic steroids in an attempt to improve their strength, speed, and power. According to the American College of Sports Medicine, use of steroids by normal, healthy people under age 50 does not in itself improve performance. The prolonged use of steroids can have a number of severe and detrimental side effects, such as liver failure, changes in libido, mood swings, aggressive behavior, and cardiovascular disease. In men, steroids can decrease testicular size, reduce sperm production, and cause breast enlargement. In women, steroids can disrupt the menstrual cycle and cause acne, male pattern baldness, growth of facial hair, and irreversible deepening of the voice.

• **Exercise and menstruation.** Not only is it safe to exercise while menstruating, but many women find that exercise helps reduce painful or uncomfortable menstrual symptoms. Menstruation doesn't affect athletic performance; women have won Olympic gold medals during every phase of the menstrual cycle.

6

Exercising at Home

A home gym makes it easy to exercise whenever you want, in the privacy of your own home. You don't have to waste time traveling to and from a health club or skip workouts when you can't make it to the club before closing. If you're training for a favorite sport, indoor equipment can provide an excellent off-season or bad-weather alternative to regular outdoor training.

Most people can't afford to equip their own gyms with the kind of high-tech exercise machines used at some health clubs. If you don't have the money or space for industry-quality equipment, you can choose from a wide variety of household aerobic and weightlifting machines that have been scaled down in both size and price.

You could spend less than $100 and set up a basic home gym consisting of a jump rope, a mat, and some hand weights. You could spend from $200 to more than $1,000 to equip a more elaborate gym with a stationary bike or rowing machine and a set of free weights or an all-in-one exercise machine.

Before buying any equipment, consider how often you plan to use it. Stationary bikes, rowing machines, treadmills, and other aerobic devices can be used for the warm-up stage of a workout, or they can comprise the total aerobic workout. The more you plan to use a piece of equipment, the more important quality becomes.

When comparing various exercise machines, don't waste your time looking at "passive" devices driven by electric motors, with belts, shakers,

or rollers that promise to "massage the inches away." These machines don't work. The only way to remove fat is to reduce your caloric intake, expend more calories through aerobic exercise, or both. Neither a machine nor a person can shake, squeeze, or rub fat off you.

Whenever possible, rent or borrow equipment for a trial period before you buy. Ask yourself whether or not you'll use the equipment faithfully. An exercise bike or rowing machine isn't going to do you any good if it sits in the closet and collects dust.

Stationary Bicycles

You can enjoy most of the benefits of outdoor cycling by pedaling a stationary bike indoors. Stationary cycling is easy for people who are uncoordinated and kind to those who are out of shape. It provides an excellent aerobic workout, strengthens the legs, builds muscular endurance, and makes certain leg and hip muscles more flexible. Indoor cycling isn't as strenuous as outdoor cycling, since you don't have to propel your body weight or overcome wind resistance. It's an excellent activity for the elderly and for rehabilitation of hip and leg injuries, because the amount of work done can be controlled.

Riding a stationary bike is similar to riding a bike with the brakes on. You pedal against some form of resistance to move the bike's single flywheel. You can adjust the resistance by regulating

Stationary Bike

How to Get a Good Workout If You Have Back Problems

If you have back problems and you are using a stationary bicycle, you can avoid pressure on your back by removing the seat and sliding a chair just behind the bike. You pedal by pushing your legs forward, and your back is supported by the chair.

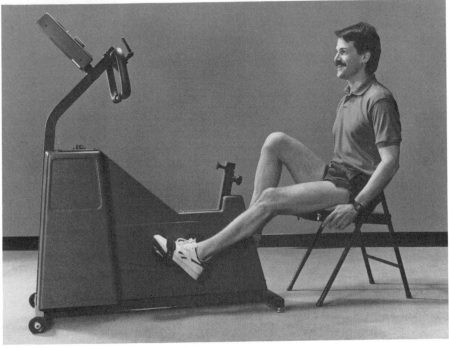

Shopping for a Stationary Bike

There are more than 100 different brands and models of exercise bikes to choose from, ranging in price from about $50 for a collapsible bike to thousands for computerized models. Whether you choose a high-tech machine or a basic bike, look for these features in a stationary bike:

• A sturdy, rigid frame that won't flex when you pedal.

• A weighted flywheel that glides with even, steady force as you pump the pedals. On cheaper bikes, the flywheels sometimes look like spoked wheels on regular bikes. These wheels tend to offer a rough ride. As a rule, the heavier the flywheel, the smoother the ride.

• A well-made flywheel. Flywheels that aren't perfectly round tend to pulsate and make it difficult to maintain a steady, rhythmic pedaling speed.

• Adjustable resistance and easy-to-reach controls. The controls on some bikes are so low on the frame you have to stop pedaling to adjust them.

• An adjustable, well-padded seat. Since on a stationary bike you rest your weight almost entirely on your seat instead of distributing your weight across the seat, handlebars, and pedals, you'll appreciate the comfort of a wide, well-padded seat. Seats are generally mounted either with a spring-loaded pin, a clamp, or a screw-in pin. Screw-in pins are least likely to slip.

• A bike that coasts. On some bikes, the pedals keep moving as long as the flywheel spins. This can be dangerous: If your foot slips off a pedal, the pedal can strike you hard in the leg. It's also easier to start pedaling if you can back-pedal to a comfortable position.

• Adequate meters. Most bikes come equipped with odometers to tell you how "far" you've pedaled and either a speedometer or a tachometer to tell you how "fast" you're pedaling. You should pay attention to your heart rate and the time you ride. You might find it useful to have a bike with a timer.

• Toe straps. These prevent your feet from slipping off the pedals and enable you to work on the upstroke as well as the downstroke. Weighted pedals are convenient. The straps stay on top, allowing you to slide your foot in more easily.

the tension of a belt cinched around the wheel or by changing the pressure of a brake pad pressed against the wheel. This makes the bike easier or harder to pedal.

During your workout, set the resistance so that you can comfortably pedal at 80 to 90 revolutions per minute (rpm). Don't set the resistance too high. You'll get a better aerobic workout and your knees will suffer less stress if you pedal faster with less resistance. Remember to check your pulse about halfway through your workout. Adjust your pedaling speed to bring you up or take you down to your target heart rate in your exercise benefit zone. (See pages 12–14.)

If you plan to make stationary cycling the aerobic portion of your fitness routine, you need to pedal for 20 to 30 minutes at 60 to 85 percent of your target heart rate at least three times a week. Start your program at a low resistance setting. As you get stronger, increase the resistance, but continue pedaling at 80 to 90 rpm.

You can find exercise bikes for less than $100, or you can spend thousands of dollars for a computerized bike that lets you ride a programmed course of simulated hills and flats. If you want to get a high-quality, basic bike, you'll probably have to spend about $250 or more. At the upper end of the price range, you're often paying for gadgetry as well as mass and metal. You could spend more for the high-tech gadgetry, but it's not necessary. It won't make exercise any easier. One common extra is an ergometer, a device that measures how hard you're working. The ergometer, which sometimes lends its name to the whole machine, lets you know how much energy you're using. Take your pulse during exercise; don't rely on an ergometer to tell you how hard to work.

Make sure the bike you choose fits you properly, or you run the risk of developing knee problems. Try the bike on for size. The bicycling section in chapter 4 (see page 22) explains how to adjust a bike to fit you properly.

Rowing Machines

Rowing machines simulate the motion of sculling. The rowing machine handles serve as oars, and your feet usually strap into footrests so you can use your legs to slide the seat back and forth as you row.

Rowing machines provide a good aerobic workout, strengthen muscles, and build flexibility in your arms, shoulders, abdominals, legs, buttocks, and back. Rowing is good, all-around exercise. If you're overweight, you might find rowing less punishing to your legs and back than other exercises because you exercise while sitting down.

Rowing isn't as easy as it looks, however. It requires a fair amount of coordination to row properly. Correct form is critical. While rowing, keep your back *straight* and don't lean back too far at the end of a stroke. Push back with your legs first, then pull the oars in. On the return stroke, first let the oars go back, then pull yourself forward, bending the knees. Practice your stroke and don't row hard until you've mastered it. Long, slow oar strokes work better than short, fast strokes. If rowing with proper form causes back strain, stop and choose another exercise.

There are three basic types of rowing machines: piston machines, oarlock rowers, and flywheels.

1. **Piston machines** usually have two arms that move back and forth in a horizontal plane. Hydraulic pistons that look like automobile shock

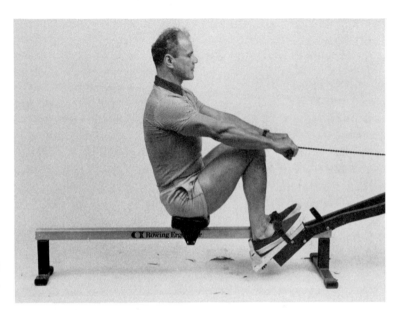

How to Use a Rowing Machine Safely

Start a stroke on a rowing machine with your back straight and your arms extended. Push with your legs.

Finish the stroke by pulling your arms to your sides and extending your legs. Do not lean backward or arch your back.

absorbers provide resistance. Piston machines are compact and easy to store. They can cost from $60 to more than $350.

2. **Oarlock rowers** have arms that pivot freely from brackets on the sides of the machine. A friction or hydraulic device provides resistance. It can be a challenge to master your stroke on an oarlock machine because the side-mounted oars are generally bulkier than those on piston machines. Most oarlock rowers cost from $170 to about $400.

3. When you row a piston or an oarlock rower, the machine stops when you do. When you row a **flywheel rower,** you work up momentum on a spinning flywheel. When you stop, the flywheel glides, simulating a scull gliding across water. To change resistance, you change the gearing of the wheel. Flywheel rowers have smooth, even action, but cost about $600 or more.

Some marketers claim their rowing machines can be used for other exercises as well. In most cases, the "multigym" rowers compromise quality as rowers in an attempt to do more. If you want a rowing machine, buy a quality rower; if you want a multigym, buy a quality gym.

If rowing is the primary component of your aerobic routine, work up to rowing the standard 20 to 30 minutes at 60 to 85 percent of your target heart rate. You'll benefit most by setting a low to moderate resistance and using a high number of strokes per minute. When you're getting started, focus on your form and increasing the time exercised. As you master the correct form and grow stronger, you can add resistance.

Shopping for a Rowing Machine

When buying a rowing machine, look for these features:

• *Sturdy construction. The lightweight tracks on many models flex under the weight of an average-sized person. The frame should be heavy enough so that it won't jump or crawl across the floor as you row.*

• *Comfortable seats that roll smoothly on ball bearings. Simple rollers move freely when there's only a little weight on them, but when someone sits on the seat the friction makes the seat stick.*

• *Proper fit. Try on a rower before you buy, to make sure you can fully extend your legs when you stroke. The handles should be in the right position so that you don't have to lean too far forward at the beginning of a stroke.*

• *Timers. Many rowing machines have timers built into the frame. A convenient timer can help you work out for the appropriate length of time, 25 or 30 minutes.*

• *Stroke counters. Some models have built-in stroke counters. They aren't necessary, but they can help you maintain your rhythm as you row.*

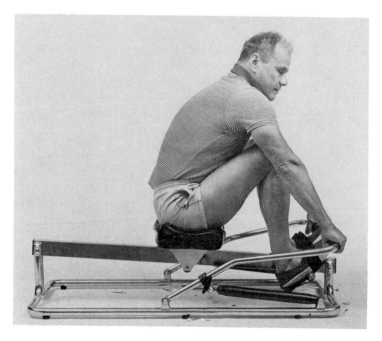

The Wrong Way to Use a Rowing Machine

The ankles are bent too severely, and the body is arched forward, causing back strain.

Cross-country Ski Machine

Cross-country Ski Machines

You can get an excellent aerobic workout from a cross-country ski machine by rhythmically pumping your arms while sliding the mechanical skis back and forth along the machine's tracks, rollers, or channels. This distinctive scissoring motion of simulated cross-country skiing can be arduous, since your arms and legs move constantly. Like rowing machines, cross-country ski machines work the upper body. In addition, they take the shoulders and hip joints through a wider range of motion, making these machines even better than rowing machines at increasing flexibility.

Ski machines have tension adjustments to change the resistance of the mechanical skis and poles. When you're getting started, set the resistance low until you get used to the sliding motion and your ski technique improves. If you use a cross-country ski machine for the aerobic portion of your workout, try to exercise for at least 20 to 30 minutes at 60 to 85 percent of your target heart rate. The Swedish word *fartlek* had its origins in cross-country skiing technique. It means "speed play," and is a good way for those in good condition to vary their routines. See page 21 for a full description of the technique.

---

*Shopping for a
Cross-country Ski Machine*

You can find ski machines for about $150 or so, but you'll probably have to spend $400 or more to find one with skis that glide smoothly. When shopping for a cross-country ski machine, look for these features:

* *Skis that slide smoothly and firmly. Test the machine; the skis on many machines tend to stick, screech, or wobble.*
* *A rigid, sturdy frame.*
* *Skis that move back and forth independently. On some ski machines, the foot pads are connected to each other by pulleys that automatically alternate—when one foot pad slides forward, the other moves back. You'll get a better workout if you have to push and pull your feet independently in both directions.*
* *Foot security. You don't want your feet to slide off the foot pads. Foot straps provide the most secure toeholds.*
* *Adjustable ski poles. The height and resistance of the poles should be adjustable.*
* *Ease of adjusting resistance. Some machines make you stop exercising and get off the machine just to adjust the tension. Look for a machine that's easy to adjust while exercising.*

Treadmills

When you want to jog but can't get outside, you can work out on a treadmill, a belt that moves at a fixed speed, forcing you to walk, jog, or run to keep up. Some treadmills can be adjusted to simulate walking or jogging uphill. Treadmill running is somewhat easier than outdoor running, since the belt propels your foot backward, but you can still get a good workout on a treadmill. Treadmills come in both motorized and non-motorized versions, but both are expensive. Motorized treadmills cost more, usually over $1,500, but they make it easier to run at a steady pace.

Extra money spent on a high-quality treadmill may be money well spent. Treadmills are fairly complicated pieces of equipment, more prone to breakdown than a stationary bicycle or a rowing machine, for example. If a treadmill breaks down, it is unusual for a repairperson to make a house call. In addition, treadmill parts are expensive, particularly for programmable, computerized units. A reliable machine can reduce the likelihood of problems causing you inconvenience. When purchasing, ask about the warranty; a service contract can be a worthwhile investment. A reputable dealer will offer a service contract in the sale. Be sure to read the warranty and the service contract carefully.

Treadmill

If you plan to make treadmill running the aerobic component of your exercise routine, run for 20 to 30 minutes at 60 to 85 percent of your target heart rate. The tips listed in the running and walking sections of chapter 4 (pages 18–22) can help you work out safely.

Rebounders

If you want to run indoors but can't afford a treadmill, you might consider buying a rebounder or mini-trampoline. Rebounders consist of a mat about 34 to 40 inches in diameter, suspended six to nine inches off the floor by springs attached to a heavy frame. They absorb up to three-fourths of the shock of landing, so they're popular for aerobic dancing as well as indoor running.

If you have high blood pressure or heart disease, do not do rebounder workouts. Bouncing on a rebounder elevates your blood pressure faster than jogging or doing aerobic routines on the ground.

Rebounding may provide sufficient exercise if

Shopping for a Treadmill

Before buying a treadmill, take a long run on the model you're considering and see how you feel the next day. Some people find that treadmill running bothers their legs.

When shopping for a treadmill, look for these features:

- *A sturdy frame.*
- *A bed that provides steady footing.*
- *Side rails or bars at your sides to help you keep your balance.*
- *On a manual treadmill, look for treads that won't slip off center.*
- *On a motorized treadmill, look for easy-to-reach controls so that you can adjust your speed or elevation without straining.*
- *Read the warranty carefully; ask the dealer about service contracts.*

Rebounder

All-in-One Gyms and Free Weights

Both all-in-one gyms and free weights can be used to develop muscle strength and endurance by working against progressively greater resistance or heavier weight. With all-in-one or multipurpose gyms, the resistance is usually provided either by springs or by a series of weight stacks connected by a pulley-and-cable system. With free weights, the resistance is provided by metal or cement-filled discs.

Many people find all-in-one machines easier to use than free weights. When using a weight machine, you can't drop a barbell on your chest or a dumbbell on your foot, and you have cams or pulleys to help you control the weight. Free weights,

you're overweight or out of shape, but if you're in good shape it might be hard for you to work up to your target heart rate on a rebounder. It takes a lot more work to jog or jump on the ground than on a rebounder.

If you want to make rebounding part of your aerobic routine, you have to jump or jog for 20 to 30 minutes at 60 to 70 percent of your target heart rate at least three times a week. If you have trouble elevating your heart rate, try swinging your arms or lifting them up and down as you jog in place.

Shopping for a Rebounder

Most rebounders cost from $50 to $100. If you're going to buy a rebounder, look for one that has these features:
- *A large-surface mat.*
- *Heavy-duty springs.*
- *A heavyweight frame that won't creep across the floor as you jump.*

All-in-One Gyms

Shopping for an All-in-One Gym

Health-club-quality weight machines cost $1,000 and up. More modest machines usually cost from $200 to $500 or so.

When shopping for a weight machine, look for these features:

• A sturdy frame with solidly welded joints. Look for a gym with few bolts and more welded joints.

• Thick padding on the bench.

• Adjustable resistance.

• A variety of exercise stations. Make sure the machine exercises all the major muscle groups: the chest, the legs, and the abdominals.

• If a machine has a pulley, choose cables made of steel. Plastic or aluminum pulleys may damage more easily.

• Make sure all components of the machine work smoothly.

• Most machines are built to accommodate someone five feet five inches to six feet tall; if you're tall or short, be sure to try out a gym before you buy.

All-in-one gyms and free weights don't provide aerobic conditioning unless you design an interval circuit training program. The section on weight training in chapter 4 (see page 25) can help you set up a program that works on aerobic fitness.

Shopping for Free Weights

Expect to pay about $35 for a set of one-, three-, five-, and 10-pound pairs of hand weights, also known as dumbbells. A deluxe chrome-plated set can cost $100 or more; consider carefully whether for you the aesthetics of chrome weights are worth the price. Using hand weights, you can do a great deal with very little equipment. If you're starting out, you may want to buy only the lighter, five-pound-and-under pairs first, and purchase heavier weights as you get stronger and need them.

Prices for barbell weights range from about $75 for a 110-pound set to about $300 for a 300-pound set. You'll probably want to buy a sturdy, well-padded bench, too. Some benches come with a rack for chest presses or a curl unit for leg work, or both.

When shopping for free weights, keep these features in mind:

• Choose weights made of steel rather than cast iron or cement-filled plastic. Steel is sturdier.

• Pairs of solid, cast hand weights are more convenient to use than sets that require you to change weights and tighten collar nuts.

• Look for knurled or textured bars; they're easier to grip than smooth bars. Try them out to make certain they don't dig into your palms.

• Choose a bench that's no more than 11 inches wide. A wider bench can interfere with movement. Check that the bench padding is sufficient for comfort, between one and two inches thick.

• Make sure the collars fasten tightly to the bar, or the weights could slip off while you're exercising. Screw collars are the safest.

on the other hand, offer other advantages: they can be used for a number of exercises not included on most weight machines, they take up much less space than weight machines, and they cost a lot less.

Unless you are using hand weights, always have another person present, a "spotter," when working out with free weights; *never* work out alone. If you work out alone with free weights, severe muscle damage, broken bones, and even death by asphyxiation, due to a crushed windpipe for example, can result if you should get into trouble. If you're likely to work out on your own, consider purchasing an all-in-one gym or hand weights only.

If you choose to work out alone with hand weights, you may want to exercise in front of mirrors to check your form. Good form is essential for good results. You can use a full-length mirror on the back of a door, or a large mirror on a bureau, if you don't want to set up a mirror in your home gym area. With free weights on a barbell, a mirror can also be useful and your spotter can monitor your form as well.

Athletic Shoes

The all-purpose sneaker is out of step with today's exercise enthusiasts, who wear a different pair of shoes for every sport. No matter what type of footwear you're looking for, make sure the shoe has arch and heel support.

Most athletic shoes are designed for a particular activity:

Aerobic shoes are lightweight and tend to have low heels with rounded edges and extra support for quick side-to-side moves. They often come in high-top versions to protect the ankles.

Baseball shoes have long tongue flaps that cover the laces to keep dust out. The soles have molded plastic or hard rubber cleats for traction.

Biking shoes are snug, light, and have no cushioning. The hard plastic soles have grooves or cleats to help grip the pedals. Use them only for biking; most biking shoes have no tread, so they're not safe for walking.

Racquetball or squash shoes have sticky soles with rounded edges that are good for traction on polished courts. The soles are thinner and more flexible than those on tennis shoes.

Running shoes are designed to move forward. They should cushion and cup your heel, support your arches, protect the ball of your foot, and flex easily in the forefoot so you don't lose momentum as you push off with your toes.

Tennis shoes tend to be heavier and stronger than other court shoes. They have flat soles and hard, squared-off edges for lateral support.

Walking shoes are lightweight and breathable. They should have flexible soles.

Exercise Extras

These exercise accessories can be used to tone specific muscle groups or to supplement your regular aerobic routine.

Chest crushers exercise the chest muscles (pectorals) by providing resistance as you press your palms together in front of your chest. Chest crushers used to be promoted heavily in the back pages of male-oriented magazines as devices capable of rapidly developing a "manly" chest for their users. For good reason, they're no longer as heavily advertised. In fact, chest crushers have only a limited use and are not a good buy in exercise equipment.

If you use a chest crusher, be sure to breathe steadily; some people hold their breath as they perform this type of isometric exercise. Because chest crushers tone the muscles that support the breasts, some marketers try to promote these devices to women as "bust developers." Don't be duped; exercise alone cannot increase breast size.

Chinning bars provide a convenient way to do chin-ups to enhance strength and endurance in your arms, chest, upper back, and trunk. Chinning bars have a tendency to serve more as clothes racks than as exercise devices. Before you buy, assess how important to you developing upper-body strength is as a performance goal. If it's important and you think you'd use one regularly, chinning bars are effective, and a reasonably good value.

You can mount a homemade bar in the rafters of your attic or in your basement, or you can buy a bar that mounts on the wall or fits in a doorway. Make certain the bar is mounted securely before you use it; some bars that mount in doorways have a tendency to slip.

Grip exercisers are sprung isometric devices

Tips on Buying Athletic Shoes

- *You should be able to wiggle your toes while standing or sitting.*
- *The shoes should bend where your foot bends.*
- *The shoes should be comfortable from the first wearing; you shouldn't have to "break them in."*
- *The inner seams shouldn't rub against your feet.*
- *The collar should hug your foot, not press into your ankle.*
- *Stand on your tiptoes. If the heels slide, the shoes don't fit.*
- *Try on both shoes. Wear the kind of socks you'll wear in your sport. If you wear orthotic inserts, take them with you and fit them in the shoes you're considering.*
- *Generally, shoes made for men don't fit women quite right. Women tend to have higher arches and narrower heels than men. If they're available, buy shoes designed for your sex.*
- *Wear your shoes only for the activity for which you bought them, or you'll lose cushioning and traction too quickly.*

you hold in your hand and squeeze to strengthen your grip. Squeezing a rubber ball or manipulating a soft, pliable substance such as plastic clay, Silly Putty, or an artist's kneaded rubber can strengthen your grip much better—and at much lower cost. Caution: These devices can dramatically raise your diastolic blood pressure.

Chest spring expanders consist of a series of steel springs attached to handles. You pull the handles apart against the springs' resistance to develop muscular strength and endurance in your arms, chest, shoulders, and upper back. Like chest crushers, spring expanders have limited value.

Hand, wrist, and ankle weights add to your work load and, when used safely, increase your strength and aerobic fitness. They usually weigh between one and ten pounds and are either hand-held or strapped around your wrists or ankles.

Use ankle weights when walking only. Never use ankle weights when running. Ankle weights significantly increase the chance of injury when running; they increase impact stress and decrease joint flexibility. Similarly, ankle weights should not be used in any exercise that increases stress on the leg joints, including rope jumping and aerobic exercise routines. Hand or wrist weights can safely be used when either walking, running, or during any aerobic exercise in which the hands are free. Such weights increase aerobic fitness by making the upper body muscles work harder than they would without them. Caution: The use of hand, wrist, or ankle weights significantly increases the intensity of the cardiovascular workout.

Start by using one-pound weights; don't add too much weight too soon. The five-pounders that feel light in the store will feel a great deal heavier after a half-hour workout. Starting with lighter weights also gives your body a chance to adjust to the additional stress.

Personal Trainers

Some people stay motivated for their workouts by hiring personal trainers. If you hire a trainer, you'll get plenty of individual attention, but expect to pay from $25 to $100 per one-hour workout. In many cases you can hire a trainer for three or four sessions to help you design and learn a fitness program, then you can work out on your own. You don't necessarily need continuing supervision and guidance to keep working, just self-discipline. In most cases, the trainers will provide all the tapes, exercise mats, and equipment needed for your workout.

Before hiring a trainer, consider your fitness goals and interests. You want to hire a trainer who can help you achieve your performance goals. You don't want to hire one who specializes in bodybuilding and weightlifting if you're really interested in stretching and aerobic exercise routines.

To find a trainer, call the physical medicine and rehabilitation department of your local hospital, or a fitness center, a dance school, or the physical education department of a local college. Or check the yellow pages.

Take precautions when hiring a person who will be entering your home. It can be difficult to determine if a personal trainer knows what he or she is doing. Before hiring a trainer, ask about his or her certification. A trainer should be certified in cardiopulmonary resuscitation (CPR), and should have some kind of certification of competence, such as the credentials held by a registered physical therapist (RPT) or by a certified athletic trainer (CAT). A college degree in exercise physiology or physical education, or certification from a fitness organization such as the American College of Sports Medicine, the Aerobics Fitness Association of America, the International Dance-Exercise Association, or the Institute for Aerobic Research are good signs of competence.

Ask for references and check them. Of course, the best references come from friends and associates who have used the trainer and can give you specifics about his or her experience. You can also check with your local Better Business Bureau, state division of consumer affairs, and state attorney general's office to see if any complaints have been lodged or legal actions initiated against the person.

Ask about rates and comparison-shop. It may well be worth paying more for a qualified trainer you feel will work better with you, but check that his or her rates are at least within reason for your area. Come to an understanding and an agreement about rates and payment before you start.

Find out what form of payment is acceptable, check or cash. Most professionals ask for payment after each session; a regular customer may eventually work out payment by the week. Don't commit yourself to multiple sessions before you have tried the trainer on a trial basis. If you're dissatisfied with the initial session, however, do not feel compelled to schedule more. If unsure, try only a session or two more. A reputable trainer will not employ hard-sell or shady sales tactics.

Expect and give common courtesy. Expect the trainer to be on time, to work efficiently and effectively, and to respect your privacy. Extend the same courtesies to the trainer.

A good trainer should be able to design a safe exercise program exactly suited to your needs and interests. If you decide to go to the expense of hiring a trainer at all, do your research to help ensure yourself a rewarding experience.

Home Videocassettes

Although a home video exercise tape can motivate you (at least for a while), provide you with some instruction, and give you a sense of companionship, consider the workout itself carefully before using a videocassette, especially if you plan to make the tape the primary component of your exercise program. A review of some of the most popular exercise videos showed that many home video exercise programs had flaws, some had serious problems, and all had a drawback inherent to the home video format: since they are self-supervised programs, some people tend to work out too hard, while others do not work hard enough.

The aerobic exercise segments of many of the home videos were not long enough to provide an adequate aerobic workout. Most were far too short; few of them gave the viewer a chance to monitor his or her pulse rate and adjust the intensity of the workout. Therefore, you may not exercise long enough or hard enough to do yourself any good, or you may work so hard that you exceed your exercise benefit zone and increase the chance of hurting yourself. In addition, not all of the videocassette routines provided a sufficient warm-up or cool-down; few gave any cool-down at all.

Neglecting these important segments of a workout increases the chance of injury. A few video routines showed models performing aerobic dance on unresilient surfaces—a dangerous practice.

Other videocassette routines involved dangerous techniques that can lead to injury, or promoted misinformation, which can yield poor results. A few videos had stretches that required the user to bounce or use sudden, abrupt movements—technically known as *ballistic stretching*—usually without adequate warm-up or, worse, as part of the warm-up itself. Ballistic stretching poses the greatest risk of injury when done as part of a warm-up, but even when one is warmed up, injuries can result if these stretches are done with incorrect form. Ballistic stretches are not really necessary at any point during an exercise routine; other exercises can stretch you better and more safely. In general, avoid exercise tapes and routines that use ballistic stretches.

Tips for Using a Videocassette Exercise Tape

• *Wear either tennis or aerobic dance shoes that provide lateral support and adequate cushioning. Do not exercise in bare feet unless the video workout involves only stretching. Never exercise in socks; they do not provide proper traction.*

• *Work out on a carpet. Never exercise on an unyielding surface.*

• *Clear the area around the television. Make certain you have enough space so that you don't strike or trip over any furnishings.*

• *Exercise in a well-ventilated area. Open windows to provide cross-ventilation or turn on an air conditioner. Never exercise in an area from which heat and humidity cannot escape.*

• *If the aerobic exercise routine does not explicitly provide a time-out to monitor your heart rate, use the Stop or Pause button about halfway through the session and take your pulse on your own. Adjust the intensity of your workout to your own target heart rate.*

• *Work at your own pace; be aware of your own fitness level. Do not try to compete with the instructor or models.*

• *Exercise videos usually work best when used for variety in conjunction with other activities.*

A few videos showed exercises that forced joints to move beyond their normal range of motion. This is known as *hyperflexion* when the joint is moved too far in the direction it's supposed to move in, and *hyperextension* when the joint is moved too far against its natural motion. An exercise that requires extreme joint hyperflexion or hyperextension can cause serious injury; do not follow a video routine that shows such exercises.

Finally, some of the tape instructors seemed to be promoting such misconceptions as spot reduction or exercising to the point of pain.

If you want to try a home videocassette workout, rent and watch the tape from start to finish *before* doing the routine. Have a pad, a pencil or pen, and a watch or stopwatch on hand. Take notes as you review the tape. Make sure the program offers a safe workout appropriate to your fitness level by checking the following:

1. **General review.** Watch for and avoid routines involving ballistic stretching, movement that requires hyperflexion or hyperextension, aerobic dancing on unresilient surfaces, the use of improper footwear, or any of the other problems mentioned above.

2. **A safe and thorough warm-up routine.** The warm-up should include, first, no more than two to three minutes of moderate exercise to increase the volume of blood circulating to the muscles, then exercises that stretch all the major muscle groups in the upper body, torso, and legs. A thorough warm-up or cool-down routine takes about 10 to 15 minutes or more.

3. **Adequate aerobic exercise.** The aerobic portion of the workout should continue for 20 to 30 minutes. The exercise must be vigorous enough for you to maintain your target heart rate in the exercise benefit zone (see chapter 3), but not so intense that you must force and strain to keep up. A built-in time-out in the program to monitor heart rate is a plus.

4. **An adequate cool-down.** Similar in form to the warm-up, the cool-down should include moderate exercise that allows your heart rate to slow down gradually, followed by a thorough stretching of all the major muscle groups. Many tapes lack any cool-down routine at all.

Previewing a rental tape allows you to find a videocassette workout that is safe and that appeals to you before you make an expensive purchase. It also gives you the opportunity to study correct form and technique before actually trying to do the exercises. If you plan to make video exercise a regular part of your fitness program, you may want to find two or three good tapes and use them for variety in conjunction with other activities.

7

Choosing a Health Club

It's easy to find a health club in most parts of the country, but it's not so easy to find a club that's right for you. Should you choose a racquet club, a figure salon, a "Y" organization, a hospital exercise program, or a full-service fitness facility? Do you want to join a stark, sweat-scented gym or a health club equipped with state-of-the-art computerized equipment and an Olympic-size pool?

The best way to find out is to visit a number of facilities. Comparison-shop; many clubs allow members to bring guests, so try to work out at several clubs before selecting one. Keep the following issues in mind when comparing facilities.

Health Club Evaluation

Cost of membership. Be prepared to pay several hundred dollars—sometimes as much as $1,000—to join a health club for one year. Ask if the club charges extra for towels, lockers, and special exercise classes, or for use of courts, pools, or saunas. Find out if membership fees can be paid for a full year rather than monthly or quarterly. Some clubs require a one-year contract paid in full on signing, but others discount lump-sum payments by 10 percent or more. Some clubs charge a one-time initiation fee for joining. A reputable club will be forthright about all charges.

Special deals. Be very skeptical about hyped-up introductory offers, for example two-for-one memberships, extremely low rates for two-year

memberships, six months free if you join immediately, and the like. Chances are good that a club offering those kinds of introductory enticements predicates its business on a higher volume of membership and a higher attrition rate—more members using the gym and fewer of them renewing. Consider how crowded the club would be if everyone took a two-for-one membership. How much attention will the management give to customers and facilities if it depends on a high attrition rate? If a deal seems too good to be true, it probably is.

Refunds. Some clubs will refund all or part of your money if you move or if you can't use the club because of illness. Even if a refund clause isn't part of a club's regular offer, ask if you can have one added to your contract.

Location. On some days, a long drive might be a tempting excuse to avoid working out. Make it easy on yourself: choose a health club near where you live or work. Try to pick a club that's not more than 15 minutes away, or at least near a major road or along your commuting route.

Parking. You don't want to spend your exercise time hunting for a parking space. A club should have enough parking for its members, even during the peak hours. The parking lot should be well lighted for security.

Club hours. Consider your schedule and the hours you want to exercise. Ask if the club restricts the facilities by having "men only" or "women only" training during certain hours or on certain days. Also ask if the club hours differ in the winter and summer seasons or on weekends, or if it has early-morning and late-evening hours for working people.

Type of equipment and activities. Some people have no trouble settling into an exercise routine and following the same program day after day; others crave variety. A well-equipped club should have both strengthening and cardiovascular conditioning equipment. For strength, a facility should have weight-training equipment, either free weights or weight machines, or both. For cardiovascular fitness, a facility should have some combination of stationary bicycles, rowing machines, treadmills, cross-country ski machines, and stair-climbing machines. There should be enough different kinds of equipment to provide you with variety.

Fitness testing. Some clubs require a stress test and medical clearance before you can join. A good health facility will evaluate your initial level of conditioning by conducting, free, tests for aerobic conditioning, strength, flexibility, and body composition. Once you're a member, some clubs offer periodic fitness testing. At other clubs, you're on your own. If you want a trainer to help you design a specialized fitness program, make sure qualified personnel are available to help you. Whether or not they ask, tell the staff about any medical problems you may have.

Qualifications of the staff. With some 50 organizations and institutes offering certification of competence in exercise, it's hard to know which qualifications indicate real competence. Some programs award certificates with little or no training; others require extensive instruction and testing.

The trainers should be certified in cardiopulmonary resuscitation (CPR). Look for other indicators of training, such as a degree in exercise physiology or certification by a reputable organization such as the American College of Sports Medicine, the Aerobics and Fitness Association of America, the International Dance-Exercise Association, or the Institute for Aerobic Research. Most health clubs do not employ registered physical therapists or certified athletic trainers, but if the club you are considering employs them, people with those credentials are certainly qualified. Since qualified and experienced trainers demand higher salaries, expect to pay more at most facilities with accredited personnel.

Availability of the equipment. Visit the facilities during peak hours. If there are long lines to use the weight equipment or stationary bicycles, the club is overcrowded, underequipped, or mismanaged.

Availability of the trainers. Some facilities require an appointment for assistance, while others have instructors available at all times. If you want personal attention when you're working out, choose a well-staffed club with qualified personnel. If they're offered, look in on a group class to see how crowded it seems.

Equipment maintenance. It doesn't matter that a health club has a fleet of 15 stationary cycles if only three of them work. Make sure the equipment is operational and the facilities are clean.

Saunas, steam baths, and whirlpools. Check these facilities for cleanliness. Saunas, steam baths, and whirlpools do nothing to improve fitness, but many people find them relaxing after a workout.

People with high blood pressure, heart disease, ulcers, or respiratory problems should consult a doctor before entering a hot sauna, a steam bath, or a heated whirlpool. Pregnant women should avoid them because the high temperatures can be harmful to the fetus.

Programs for special needs. Some facilities provide specialized programs for the handicapped, for cardiac patients, and for people with orthopedic problems. A growing number of clubs now offer nutrition counseling, weight-management programs, smoking clinics, and physical therapy sessions.

If you have special needs and your local health club doesn't offer any programs to meet those needs, check with your physician, hospitals, medical centers, educational institutions, and the various "Y" associations in your area.

Fitness networks. Some clubs belong to organizations and trade associations such as the International Physical Fitness Association. Sometimes these clubs offer reciprocal club privileges to members. That means you can use a facility in another area if you travel or move. In most cases, the host club will charge facility or maintenance fees, but they should be cheaper than guest fees.

Signing Up

During the first six months of membership, about half the people who join health clubs stop going. You can save yourself a lot of money if you take out a short-term trial membership before you sign an extended contract. You might not use the club enough to make a long-term membership worthwhile.

Before signing, read the contract carefully; ask questions about anything you don't understand. A reputable health club will let you take the contract home if you want to.

More than half the states have laws protecting consumers who join health clubs. These laws usually protect consumers in a number of ways:

1. They require health clubs to register and to post bond so that members can get their money back if the club goes bankrupt.
2. They limit the length of contracts, often prohibiting lifetime memberships.
3. They put a cap on membership fees.
4. They require a three-day cooling-off period that allows new members to cancel their contracts and that requires health clubs to refund all deposits and fees if a new member changes his or her mind in that time.

Most states with laws covering fitness facilities exclude certain groups, such as nonprofit organizations ("Y" organizations for instance), clubs that specialize in one sport (such as golf, tennis, or racquet clubs), and facilities that don't use exercise equipment (such as dance and aerobics studios). Call the state attorney general's office to find out exactly what laws regulate health clubs in your state.

If you aren't sure of a health club's reputation, call the local Better Business Bureau, the state attorney general's office, or the state consumer protection agency. Ask if complaints have been filed by dissatisfied club members.

8

Common Injuries
and Their Prevention

Some exercise injuries can't be prevented; for example, you can't do much to avoid getting hurt if you take a tumble on the ski slopes. But you can avoid many unnecessary injuries by following four simple precautions:

1. Warm up and stretch before exercise and cool down and stretch afterwards. Stretch thoroughly.
2. Make sure your athletic gear is designed for your sport and that it fits you properly. Tennis shoes aren't designed for jogging; jogging shoes aren't designed for aerobic exercise routines.
3. Strengthen the specific muscles used in your sport to avoid overuse injuries. Shinsplints, runner's knee, Achilles tendonitis, and tennis elbow are examples of common overuse injuries.
4. Know your limits and don't exceed them. Don't push yourself to the point of excessive fatigue. When you work too hard, your muscles tire and your body recruits supporting muscles to help do the work. The backup muscles have to work extra hard, and muscle strains, pulls, or joint damage may result.

First Aid

If you're injured during exercise, stop; don't "play through the pain." Technically, a muscle or tendon suffers a strain, such as a tear or pull, and a ligament in a joint suffers sprain, trauma to the ligament itself. If you strain a muscle or sprain a joint, the injury will become inflamed—painful, hot, swollen, and red. The faster you can control the inflammation, the better. It's difficult, however, for the layperson to judge the degree of strain or sprain, therefore it's advisable to seek professional medical attention or advice as soon as possible, particularly if function is impaired.

To reduce inflammation, follow the RICE rule of first aid: Rest, Ice, Compression, and Elevation. You can use two methods to ice down an injury, an ice pack or an ice massage.

To make an ice pack, wrap ice in a towel and apply the pack around the injury. Make sure the ice pack covers the entire injured area, both above and below the actual point of injury. Hold the ice pack firmly but not too tightly in place by wrapping it with either an elastic bandage or another towel. Keep the pack in place for five to ten minutes, remove it for five to ten minutes, then reapply it for another five to ten minutes. Elevate the injury during this process. Wrap the injury in an elastic bandage. Rest and keep the injury elevated as much as possible afterward.

An ice massage is a very effective method of controlling swelling. You must have a paper cup filled with ice prepared in your freezer. (Use the ice-pack method if you don't have a cup full of ice ready.) Peel away the top of the cup and massage the entire injured area with the exposed ice. Always massage above and below the injury itself, particularly if a joint is injured. Ice-massage for five to ten minutes, elevate the injury for five to ten minutes, then massage again for five to ten minutes. Wrap the injury with an elastic bandage. Rest and keep the injury elevated as much as possible afterward.

A physician may direct you to repeat either of the above treatments periodically, anywhere from once an hour to once every three or four hours, throughout the next 48 hours.

Follow these rules when injured:

1. Stop exercising immediately.
2. As soon as possible, follow the RICE rule with either an ice pack or ice massage.
3. Consult a physician to determine the extent of the injury.

After you've been injured, don't return to your exercise routine until all symptoms and pain have stopped and a physician has cleared you to start exercising again. Sometimes non-weight-bearing activities, such as swimming and bicycling, can be used to maintain conditioning during the recovery period. Start by strengthening both the injured muscle and the surrounding muscles. Work slowly and gradually to build up to your pre-injury workout intensity. Recovery from severe injuries should be done under professional medical supervision.

Prevention is the most important aspect of injury control. Warm up, cool down, and stretch thoroughly. The following exercises are designed to prevent injury. Pay particular attention to strengthening and stretching heavily used muscle groups.

Caution: Rehabilitation from an injury should be undertaken only with professional medical supervision. When cleared by your doctor to begin rehabilitation, you may want to take this book along to see if he or she recommends any of the exercises in it.

Shinsplints and Ankle Sprains

The term *shinsplints* aptly describes the pain and aching caused by inflammation of the bone covering and tendon in the front of the lower leg. You're at risk of developing shinsplints if your shin muscles, which pull your forefoot up, are weaker than your calf muscles, which pull the forefoot down. Your shin muscles are damaged when they strain to keep up with your more powerful calf muscles. Those who run or jog, jump rope, do aerobic exercise routines, play basketball or racquet sports, or exercise on unyielding surfaces should add a selection of the strengthening and stretching exercises in this section to their warm-up and cool-down to help prevent shinsplints and ankle sprains. (When possible, avoid exercising on unyielding surfaces.)

If you develop shinsplints, ice and massage the affected area. Resting a few days can ease the pain, but the discomfort is likely to return when you start exercising again. The only way to prevent shinsplints, and to avoid recurring bouts of this annoying injury, is to strengthen your shin muscles and stretch your calves. The exercises in this section are designed to do that.

Ankle injuries are more serious than shinsplints, since they involve excessive stretching or tearing of the ligaments that surround and support your ankle. If you injure an ankle, immediately follow the RICE rule of first aid described in the preceding pages. *Do not* remove your shoe until you consult a doctor who can assess the severity of the damage.

It takes several weeks for a ligament to heal completely. The exact length of time depends on the degree of damage. If you injure your ankle, you'll have to take it easy for a while. When your doctor says you can begin rehabilitating your ankle, give the following exercises a try if your doctor approves them. Generally, the rehabilitation of severe injuries such as those affecting the ankle requires professional supervision.

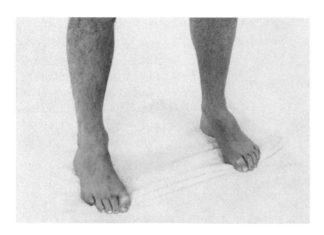

Toe Curls with a Towel

Stand tall with a towel spread out in front of your feet. Use your toes to bunch up the towel. Repeat 5 times, and gradually build to 15 times. If your feet cramp, stop exercising and point and flex your foot back and forth. When the muscles in your feet get stronger, put a 1-to-3-pound weight or heavy book at the end of the towel.

You can also strengthen your toes, feet, and shins by picking up marbles, pencils, or other small objects with your toes.

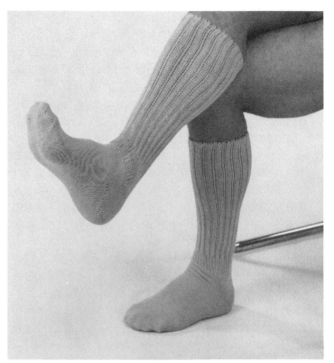

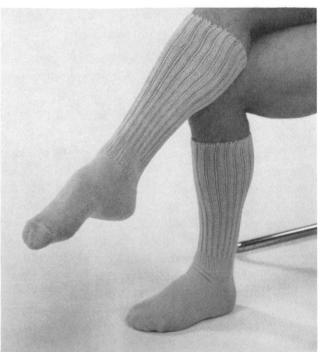

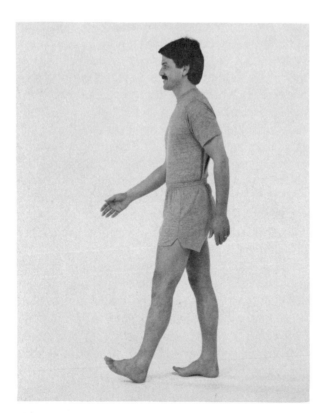

Heel Walk

Flex your feet and walk about 10 yards on your heels. Repeat 2 times, and gradually build to 5 times. Do not jam your heels down. If you develop cramps in your feet or shins, stop exercising and point and flex your feet to ease the tension.

Foot Flex

Sit in a chair, with your right leg crossed over your left. Point, then flex your foot. Repeat 10 times, then switch feet. Gradually build to 20 repetitions with each foot. After you can comfortably do 20 repetitions, add an ankle weight at the toe and repeat. Start with 10 repetitions and gradually build to 20.

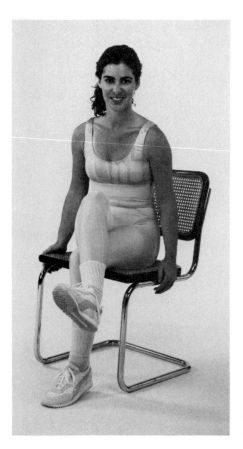
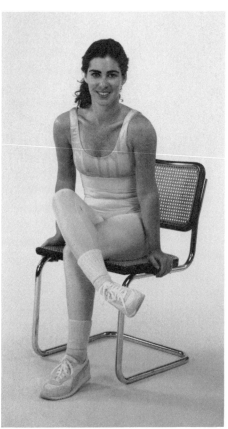

Ankle Rotation

Sit in a chair, with your right leg crossed over your left. Rotate your foot at the ankle back and forth 10 times in each direction. Repeat with the opposite ankle. Gradually build to 20 rotations in each direction.

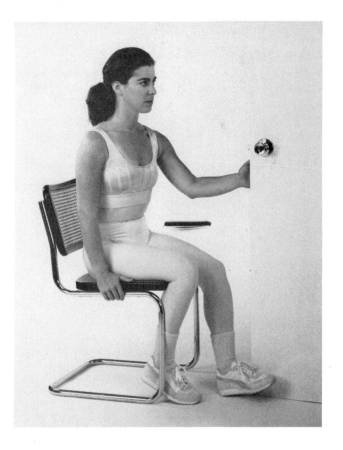

Ankle Push

Sit in a chair in front of an open door. Place the outside of your left foot against the edge of the door. Hold the door and push your foot against the door. Hold for 7 seconds. Do 5 repetitions with your left foot, then repeat the exercise with the opposite foot. Gradually build to 10 repetitions with each foot.

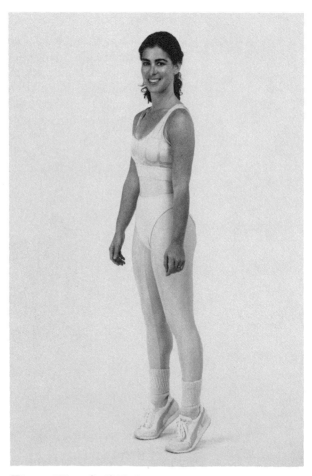

Three-Way Calf Raises

Stand with your back straight, with your knees bent slightly and your feet pointing out straight ahead of you. Raise up on the balls of your feet, then lower yourself down. Keep the motion smooth and controlled; *don't bounce.* Repeat 10 times, and gradually build to 20 repetitions.

After completing a set of calf raises with your feet pointing straight ahead of you, do two more sets, one set with your feet pointing out and one set with your feet pointing in. Do not strain when turning your feet out or in; limit the turning out and turning in to what you can do comfortably. Do 10 repetitions of the exercise each way, and gradually build to 20 repetitions.

Stress Fractures

Stress fractures are small, hairline cracks in the bones, commonly occurring in the lower legs and feet. Pain from a stress fracture in the lower leg may feel similar to the pain from shinsplints, but the pain will be sharper and more localized. A stress fracture usually hurts when you press with your finger directly above and below the area. A tender muscle tendon, as is found in shinsplints, usually hurts when pressed from one side. Sometimes, especially in the smaller foot bones, X rays may not be sensitive enough to detect stress fractures until a bony material forms over the crack— about two or three weeks after the injury.

People who run or jog, do aerobic dancing, jump rope, or play basketball are prone to stress fractures. In addition to a good warm-up, cooldown, and extra strengthening and stretching exercises, you can reduce your chances of developing stress fractures by wearing supportive footwear, by avoiding constant hard foot impact during exercise, and by using proper form when you run. Stress fractures heal by themselves in most cases.

To prevent stress fractures, stretch and strengthen your foot and ankle muscles by following the same exercises listed in the "Shinsplints and Ankle Sprains" section of this chapter, immediately preceding.

Common Knee Problems

The knee is the most commonly injured joint in sports. If you suffer a knee injury, seek medical advice immediately. Though knee sprains can be either mild or severe, an injury can be much more complicated than it initially appears. It takes a professional to accurately assess the severity of a knee injury.

Instability of the knee structure, owing to weakness of the muscles around the knees, causes many knee problems. Other causes include genetic structural problems, poor form, direct trauma to the joint, and muscle strength imbalance. Runners and people who participate in stop-and-go and contact sports are prone to knee injuries. To prevent knee injury, it's important to strengthen and stretch both your quadriceps (the muscles in the fronts of the thighs), and your hamstrings (the muscles in the backs of the thighs). The quadriceps provide essential support for the knees; the hamstrings are the primary flexors, or movers, of the knees.

The following exercises can help strengthen the muscles around the knee and help prevent injury.

The calf raises shown in the "Shinsplints and Ankle Sprains" section of this chapter will also be helpful. Rehabilitation from a knee injury should only be undertaken with professional medical supervision.

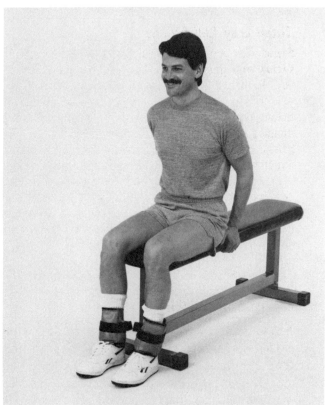

Knee Flexion/Extension

Sit on a bench with 3-to-5-pound ankle weights on and your knees extended just over the edge of the bench. Extend your right leg straight out in front of you, then lower the leg to the starting position. Keep your ankle flexed. Do 10 to 12 repetitions, then repeat the exercise with the opposite leg.

Leg Curls

Lie on your stomach on a bench, with 3-to-5-pound ankle weights on, your head relaxed to one side, and a rolled towel under your stomach to prevent back hyperextension. Extend your knees just beyond the edge of the bench, but don't hyperextend your knees. Curl your legs toward your buttocks. Keep your ankles flexed. Repeat 10 to 12 times.

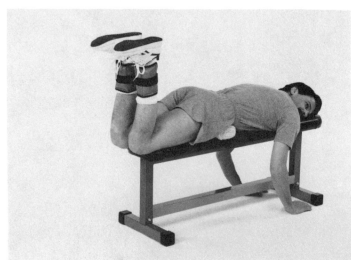

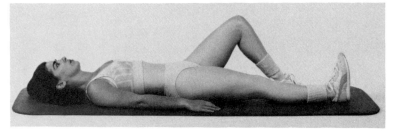

Straight Leg Raises

Lie on your back on the floor, with your left leg bent and your left foot flat on the floor. Extend your right leg straight out in front of you. Keep your right foot flexed and your lower back flat on the floor. Slowly raise and lower your right leg 10 to 12 times. Repeat with the opposite leg. Keep your lower back flat on the floor. Add one-pound ankle weights when your legs and abdomen become stronger.

Shoulder Pain

Shoulder and rotator cuff injuries are common among competitive swimmers and people who participate in racquet sports, throwing sports, and golf. People who participate in those activities can add a selection of exercises from this section to their warm-up and cool-down to help prevent injury.

If you injure your shoulder or suffer shoulder pain, try to rest the area as much as possible. Shoulder pain can also be caused by inflammatory problems such as bursitis. Consult a doctor to determine the extent of the injury and its probable cause and appropriate treatment. If you carry a briefcase or bags of groceries, use the healthy arm whenever possible; avoid using your injured arm. Because it's difficult to rest your shoulder completely, the problem is more easily prevented than cured. The following exercises are designed to strengthen and stretch the muscles and tendons in your shoulders to prevent injury.

Front Raise

Stand tall, holding a 1-to-3-pound weight in each hand. Keeping your arms straight, raise the weights in front of you until your arms are at shoulder level, parallel to the floor. Hold for 3 seconds, then lower. Repeat 10 times, and gradually build to 20 repetitions. When you can do 20 repetitions easily, increase the weights to 5 to 10 pounds and start again at 10 repetitions.

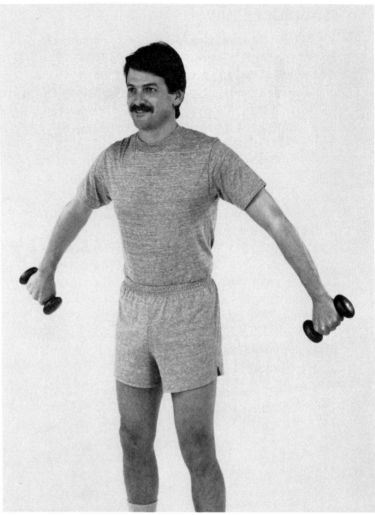

Standing Shoulder Fly

Stand tall with your arms at your sides, with a 1-to-3-pound weight in each hand. Keep your palms down and hold your arms away from your body, as shown. Keeping them away from your body, raise your arms behind you, then return them to starting position. Repeat 10 times, and gradually build to 20 repetitions. When you can do 20 repetitions easily, increase the weights to 5 to 10 pounds and start again at 10 repetitions.

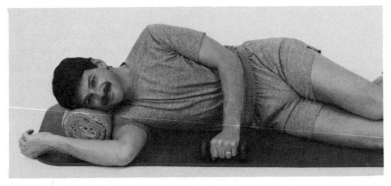

External Rotation

Lie on your side on the floor, as shown. Use a pillow or rolled-up towel to support your head. Hold your elbow close against your ribs. Holding a 1-to-3-pound weight, slowly raise the weight until it is pointed at the ceiling. Lower and repeat 10 times. Gradually build to 20 repetitions. Repeat with the opposite arm. When you can do 20 repetitions easily, increase the weight to 5 to 10 pounds.

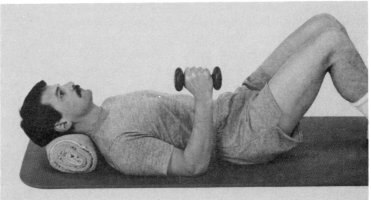

Internal Rotation

Lie on your back on the floor, with your knees bent, as shown. Use a pillow or rolled-up towel to support your head. Hold a 1-to-3-pound weight in your right hand. Keep your right elbow close against your ribs, and slowly raise the weight until it is pointed toward the ceiling. Lower and repeat 10 times. Repeat the exercise with the opposite arm. Gradually build to 20 repetitions. When you can do 20 repetitions easily, increase the weight to 5 to 10 pounds and start again at 10 repetitions.

Front Fly

Lie on your back on the floor, with your knees bent, as shown. Use a pillow or rolled-up towel to support your head. Hold a 1-to-3-pound weight in your right hand. Extend your right arm straight out from your side. Slowly raise the weight until it is pointed toward the ceiling. Lower and repeat 10 times. Repeat the exercise with your left arm. Gradually build to 20 repetitions. When you can do 20 repetitions easily, increase the weights to 5 to 10 pounds and start again at 10 repetitions.

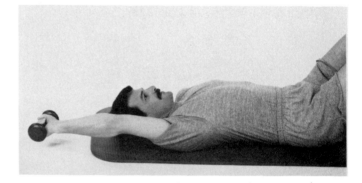

Overhead Fly

Lie on your back on the floor, with your knees bent, as shown. Hold a 1-to-3-pound weight in your right hand. Extend your right arm straight out from your head, parallel to the floor. Slowly raise the weight until it is pointed toward the ceiling. Lower and repeat 10 times. Repeat the exercise with your left arm. Gradually build to 20 repetitions. When you can do 20 repetitions easily, increase the weights to 5 to 10 pounds and start again at 10 repetitions.

Lateral Fly

Lie on your stomach on a bench, with your head relaxed to one side. Hold a 1-to-3-pound weight in your left hand. Extend your left arm down in front of you, as shown. Slowly raise the weight out to the side, keeping your arm straight until it is at shoulder level, parallel to the floor. Lower and repeat 10 times. Repeat the exercise with your right arm. Gradually build to 20 repetitions. When you can do 20 repetitions easily, increase the weights to 5 to 10 pounds and start again at 10 repetitions.

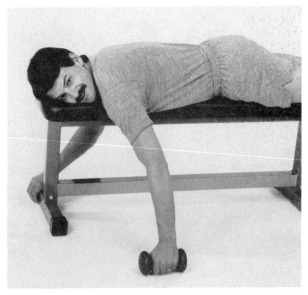

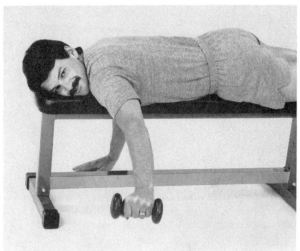

Backward Fly

Lie on your stomach on a bench, with your head relaxed to one side. Hold a 1-to-3-pound weight in your left hand. Extend your left arm down in front of you, pointed slightly toward your feet, as shown. Slowly raise the weight behind you, reaching back, until it is just above your buttocks. Keep your arm straight. Lower and repeat 10 times. Repeat the exercise with your right arm. Gradually build to 20 repetitions. When you can do 20 repetitions easily, increase the weight to 5 to 10 pounds and start again at 10 repetitions.

Tennis Elbow and Golfer's Elbow

Tennis elbow is an inflammation of the tendons that join the extensor forearm muscles to the outside (lateral) elbow. Golfer's elbow is an inflammation of the tendons that join the flexor forearm muscles to the inside (medial) elbow. Both problems are caused by overloading the forearm muscles. People who participate in throwing sports and racquet sports are prone to tennis or golfer's elbow, as are gardeners and carpenters as well.

The initial pain of both tennis elbow and golfer's elbow can be helped by massaging the painful area with a paper cup filled with ice. When the pain subsides, work on building strength, endurance, and flexibility in the tendons and muscles of your forearms. The exercises that follow can help you. A protective support strap worn around your forearm can take some of the load off the elbow joint itself.

Tennis elbow and golfer's elbow are usually the result of improper form or of weakness in the muscles surrounding the elbow. Participants who suffer from either of these disorders should consider some coaching to correct their technique. Tennis and other racquet sports players may be using a racquet that is too heavy or has an oversized grip. Check with a professional coach if you're unsure about the size of your racquet.

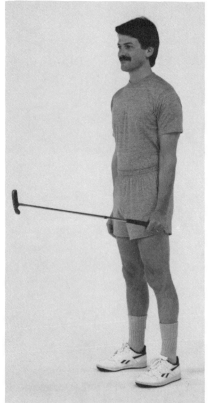
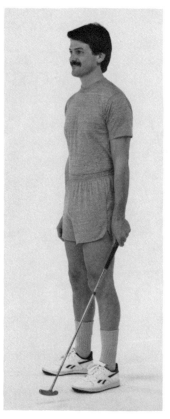

Wrist Lever Forward

Stand with your arms at your sides. Hold a golf club at the top of its grip. (A broom handle or tennis racquet may also be used.) Using only your wrist and keeping your arms straight, raise the club's head up, then lower it down. Keep the club pointed in front of you. Do 10 repetitions, then repeat the exercise with the opposite arm. As your wrists become stronger, lift a heavier object, such as a baseball bat.

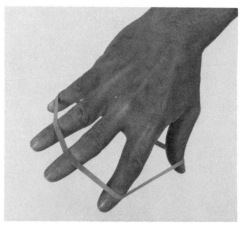

Finger Abduction

Slip a rubber band over the ends of your fingers. Separate your fingers, stretching the rubber band out as far as possible. Hold for 10 seconds. Do 10 repetitions, then repeat with the opposite hand. You can also exercise your wrist and forearm muscles by working a ball of plastic clay, Silly Putty, or artist's kneaded rubber in the palm of your hand.

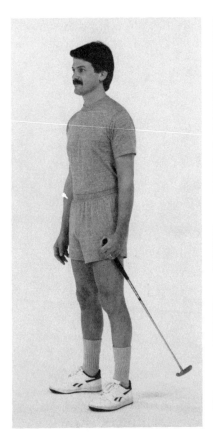

Wrist Lever Backward

Stand with your arms at your sides. Hold a golf club at the top of its grip. (A broom handle or tennis racquet may also be used.) Using only your wrist and keeping your arms straight, raise the club's head up, then lower it down. Keep the club's head pointed behind you. Do 10 repetitions, then repeat the exercise with the opposite arm. As your wrists become stronger, lift a heavier object, such as a baseball bat.

Wrist Twist (Supination and Pronation)

Stand tall and bend one arm at a 90-degree angle so that the forearm is extended out in front of you. Hold a golf club across your torso with your palm down. (A broom handle or tennis racquet may also be used.) Rotate your wrist 180 degrees. Keep your elbow at your side; use your wrists and forearms. Do 10 to 12 rotations, then repeat using the opposite arm.

Wrist Curl

Sit in a chair, with your back straight and your forearms resting on your thighs. Grip a 1-to-3-pound weight in each hand with your palms facing up. Using your forearms, flex your wrists and curl the weights. Keep your elbows and forearms down. Repeat 10 to 12 times.

Reverse Wrist Curl

Sit in a chair, with your back straight and your forearms resting on your thighs. Grip a 1-to-3-pound weight in each hand with your palms facing down. Using your forearms, extend your wrists and curl the weights. Keep your elbows and forearms down. Repeat 10 to 12 times.

Lower-Back Pain

Many people suffer from backache at some point in their lives. Though structural problems such as cracked vertebrae and damaged discs cause some lower-back pain, nearly four out of five backaches are caused by muscular problems. Tension, excess weight, and weak muscles, particularly abdominal muscles, often aggravate muscular back pain.

Your back muscles sheath and support your spine in the back, while layers of abdominal muscles support your spine in the front. When your body works in balance, the muscles pull against one another to keep your body centered on your spine. When your abdominal muscles are weak, the back muscles must support the entire weight of the upper body. The back gets pulled out of alignment, and your back muscles may tense up, resulting in back pain. Many backaches can be prevented or eliminated by stretching and strengthening back muscles and strengthening abdominals. The following exercises can help prevent or reduce lower-back pain. When you can do so without discomfort, one or more of them should be added—consistently—to your exercise program.

Seek medical advice if your pain is intense; if it radiates or creates a burning sensation; if it spreads to the lower leg or buttocks; if it lasts more than a week or two; or if it worsens in spite of bed rest.

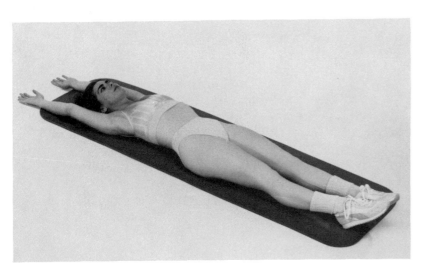

Full-Body Stretch

Lie flat on the floor, with your arms extended over your head. Stretch your arms and legs, lengthening your arms, shoulders, rib cage, abdominals, spine, legs, and feet. Breathe slowly and steadily. Hold one time for 30 seconds.

Pelvis Tilt

Lie on your back, with your knees bent and feet flat on the floor. Squeeze your buttocks together and rotate your pelvis upward. Your lower back will press on the floor. Hold the tilt for 3 to 5 seconds. Repeat 10 times.

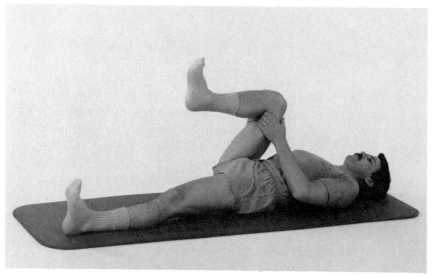

Single Leg Pull

Lie on your back on the floor, with one leg straight. Grip the other leg just behind the knee and gently pull toward your chest. Hold one time for 30 seconds. Switch knees and hold one time for another 30 seconds.

Double Knee Pull

Lie on your back with your knees bent and the soles of your feet flat on the floor. Grip both of your legs just behind your knees and draw your knees into your chest. Hold one time for 30 seconds.

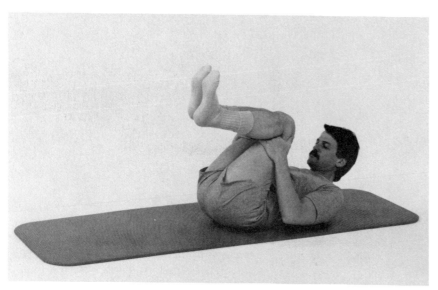

Roll-up

Lie on your back on the floor. Grip both of your legs behind your knees and tuck up into a ball. Hold one time for 30 seconds.

Lying Side Stretch

Lie on your back on the floor, with your left knee bent and your left foot flat on the floor. Cross your right leg over your left, as shown. Slowly rotate your hips as you lower your left leg toward the floor. Keep your shoulders flat on the floor. Hold one time for 30 seconds. Switch legs and hold one time for another 30 seconds.

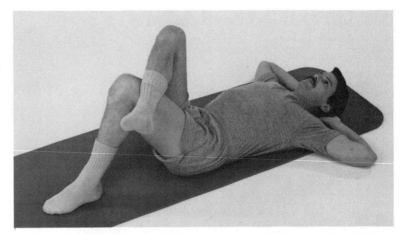

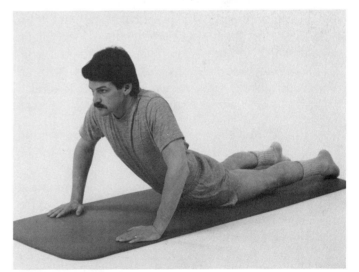

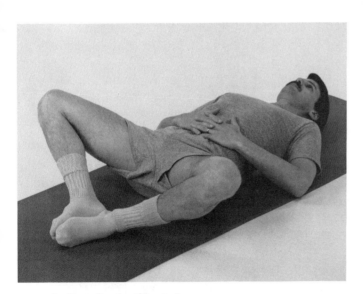

Lying Groin Stretch

Lie on your back on the floor. Put the soles of your feet together and draw your feet in toward your body. Let gravity pull your knees toward the ground. Hold one time for 30 seconds.

Back Hyperextension

Lie on your stomach on the floor. Keep your legs straight and flat on the floor. Push your upper body off the floor, keeping your hips pressed to the floor. Keep your elbows slightly bent; *don't strain*. Hold for 30 seconds, then lower. Repeat three times.

Common Injuries and Their Prevention

Other Exercise-Related Problems

Achilles Tendonitis Many people, especially runners, experience Achilles tendonitis, an inflammation of the tendon connecting the calf muscle to the heel bone. It is often caused by running on hard surfaces or wearing unstable exercise shoes.

If you develop tendonitis, ice-massage your tendon and ankle, then rest your foot. Consult with a physician to determine if you should begin to stretch your heels and ankles every day.

If you have a mild case and your physician advises you that you can continue exercising, reduce the intensity, duration, and frequency of your workouts. Then work on strengthening your tendons and supporting muscles by doing the ankle exercises listed earlier in this chapter.

Side Stitch Most runners have experienced a "stitch"—a sharp pain underneath the rib cage, usually on the right side. Whether the pain is the result of minor muscle spasms of the diaphragm or the muscles between the ribs, or whether it is caused by eating before exercise, has not been determined.

You're more likely to develop a stitch early in training or after an extended layoff, when you're out of condition. There's no way to prevent a stitch. If you develop a stitch, inhale deeply, lean forward, and press your fingertips into your side. You may also find it helpful to reach the arm on your affected side up over your head to stretch the muscles in your side.

Pulled Muscles A muscle pull or strain is an acute tear of the muscle fibers or surrounding tissue. When you pull a muscle, you'll feel a sharp, localized, and persistent pain, and you may develop a bruise. To treat a pulled muscle, apply ice to the affected area and elevate it whenever possible during the first 48 hours. After the period of rest, bathe the muscle in hot- and cold-water baths. Start with three to five minutes in hot water, followed by two minutes in cold water. Alternate between hot and cold baths for 20 minutes, starting and ending with hot baths. If the pain persists, or acute muscle tightness or skin discoloration results, you may want to consult a physician.

The best way to prevent muscle pulls is to warm up thoroughly. The stretches listed in chapter 5 can be used to stretch all your major muscle groups.

Amenorrhea If you're a woman and you exercise strenuously for prolonged time periods, you may develop amenorrhea, a condition marked by irregular or skipped menstrual periods. Doctors have not clearly defined the limits of safe exercise, but exercising in your exercise benefit zone three or four times a week for less than one hour at a time isn't likely to cause amenorrhea. Some researchers believe the problem arises when women burn too much of their stored body fat, creating a hormone imbalance. If you develop menstrual abnormalities, see your doctor.

Heat-Related Illness When your body begins to overheat during exercise, you may feel very tired and have a rapid heart rate. If you don't stop exercising and rest, this condition, known as *heat fatigue*, can develop into *heat exhaustion*. If you suffer from heat exhaustion, your body temperature will rise, your blood pressure will drop, your pulse will become rapid and weak, and your skin will grow cold and clammy. Left unchecked, your condition can further deteriorate to *heat stroke*, a medical emergency in which sweating is diminished or absent, body temperature soars to 105 degrees or higher, and skin appears hot, dry, and flushed.

Muscle cramping, nausea and vomiting, headache, dizziness, goosebumps, confusion, slurred speech, and collapse are signs of overheating. If you begin to show signs of heat-related illness, stop exercising and ask someone to apply wet compresses and crushed ice all over your body to cool you down. Act quickly, since overheating can result in brain damage or death. If there are signs of heat stroke, ask someone to call a doctor immediately.

Blisters Sooner or later, most people who exercise develop blisters. Blisters are caused by heat or friction. Shoes that fit well are the best protection against blisters. You can decrease friction when exercising by applying petroleum jelly to the blister-prone area.

If you get a blister, put a piece of adhesive tape

or a bandage over it and let it alone. If a blister pops, cover it and leave the loose skin that remains. Clean the area with alcohol or a solution of hydrogen peroxide and change the dressing twice a day. Watch for any sign of infection. When let alone, blisters heal fastest and are less likely to become infected; resist the urge to lance a blister.

Chafing   When your skin repeatedly rubs against skin or clothing, it can result in irritation or chafing. The problem is sometimes aggravated by perspiration wetness, which can make skin sticky and increase friction, especially in the inner thighs. To avoid chafing, shake powder onto the chafing-prone area before exercise to absorb perspiration, or apply petroleum jelly to cut down on friction.

9

Exercise and Older Persons

You don't need to become sedentary when you reach your sixty-fifth birthday or decide to retire. Although it's best to start exercising when you're young, and to stay fit throughout life, it's better to start exercising late in life than not at all.

As you grow older, certain changes in your body are inevitable:

1. Your aerobic capacity decreases. As you age, your heart and lungs won't be able to work quite as hard, but you can delay the decline by doing regular aerobic activity.
2. Your body composition probably changes. Whether because the body stores more fat as you age or because older people tend to be less active and therefore lose muscle mass remains unclear. Most older people, however, have a lower percentage of lean body mass—muscle, bone, and water—and a higher percentage of total body fat.
3. Your muscular strength gradually declines. Muscular strength usually peaks between the ages of 20 and 30. By age 60, most people have lost about 10 to 20 percent of their peak maximum strength.
4. You lose flexibility. Older people often ex-

perience stiffness and pain in their muscles and joints caused by the shortening and tightening of their ligaments, tendons, and muscles owing to lack of use. Regular stretching can help ease this pain.

An Exercise Routine for Older Persons

You can't stop the aging process, but you can slow it down by exercising regularly. A sensible exercise program, following the fitness fundamentals outlined in chapter 3, can help you build cardiovascular and muscular strength. Regular exercise may also help you overcome the aches and pains of osteoarthritis, the most common form of arthritis.

Before starting any exercise program, consult your doctor. If your doctor approves, then refer to chapters 3 and 4 to design your exercise program. Start slowly, and exercise at your own pace. The following stretches and the underwater exercises starting on page 27 may be good additions to your routine.

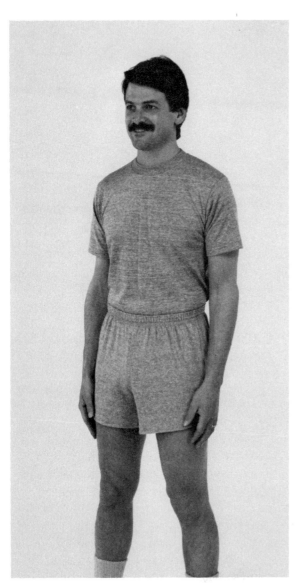 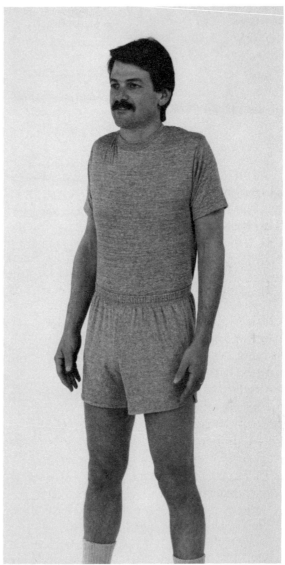

Shoulder Shrugs

Stand with your arms at your sides. Keeping your neck loose, shrug then relax your shoulders. Repeat 10 times.

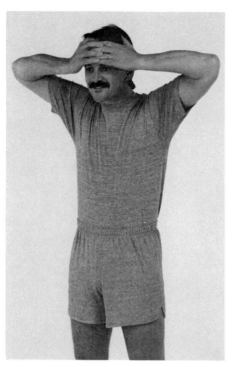  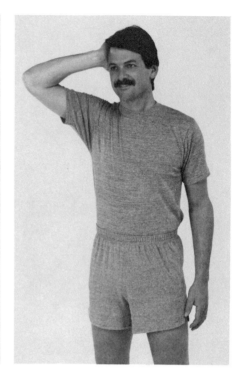

Neck Resistance

Place your hands flat across your forehead. Push your head forward against the very slight resistance of your hands. *Don't hold your breath.* Hold one time 5 to 7 seconds.

Clasp your hands behind your head. Push your head back against the very slight resistance of your hands. *Don't hold your breath.* Hold one time 5 to 7 seconds.

Hold your right hand flat against the right side of your head. Push your head to the right against the very slight resistance of your right hand. *Don't hold your breath.* Hold one time 5 to 7 seconds.

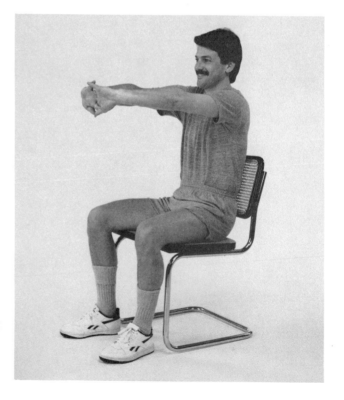

Front Arm Stretch

Interlace your fingers and straighten your arms in front of you, with your palms facing away. You should feel the stretch along the length of your arms. Hold one time for 30 seconds, then relax.

Hold your left hand flat against the left side of your head. Push your head to the left against the very slight resistance of your left hand. Don't hold your breath. Hold one time 5 to 7 seconds.

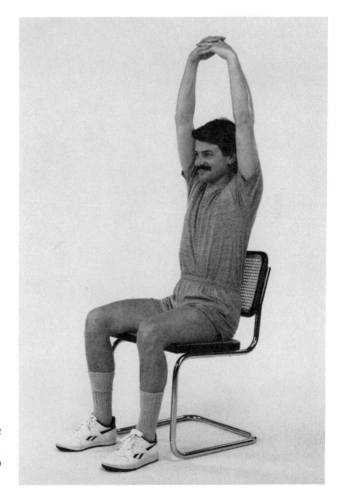

Overhead Stretch

Interlace your fingers and straighten your arms above your head, with your palms facing toward the ceiling. You should feel the stretch along your sides and up your arms. Hold one time for 30 seconds, then relax.

Side Stretch

Extend your arms overhead and clasp your hands together. Slowly lean to the right. You should feel the stretch along your left side. Hold one time for 15 to 30 seconds. Relax, then lean to the left and hold another 30 seconds.

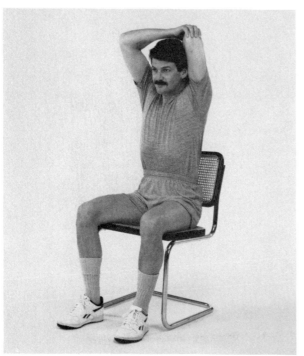

Upper Arm Stretch

Lift your left arm behind your head and hold your left elbow with your right hand. Gently push your elbow behind your head. You should feel the stretch along your upper arm. Hold one time for 30 seconds, then relax. Repeat with the other arm and hold for another 30 seconds.

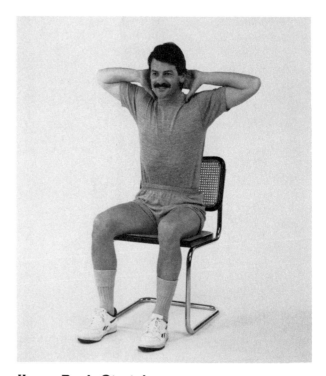

Upper Back Stretch

Interlace your fingers behind your head. Push your fingers together. You should feel the stretch across your chest and upper back. Hold one time for 30 seconds, then relax.

Lower Back Stretch

Sit in a chair and bend down to reach your toes. Lean forward with your arms between your legs. You should feel the stretch along the length of your back. Hold one time for 30 seconds, then relax. Sit up slowly.

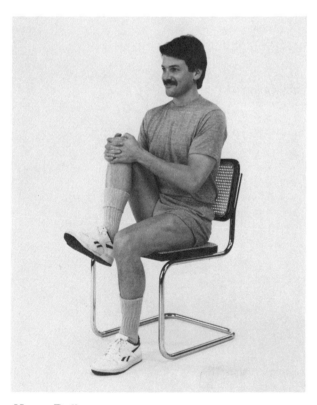

Knee Pull

Sit in a chair and grip your right leg around the knee with both hands. Gently pull your leg up and into your chest. You should feel the stretch along your hamstrings and buttocks. Hold one time for 30 seconds, then relax. Repeat with the opposite leg.

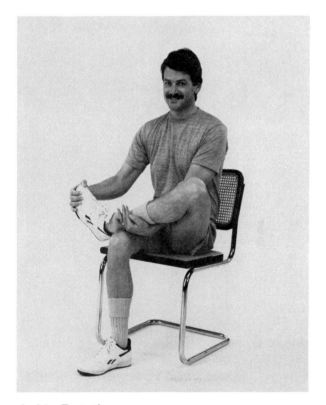

Ankle Rotation

Sit in a chair, with one leg crossed in your lap. Use your hands to rotate the ankle clockwise, then counterclockwise. Rotate 5 times in each direction, then repeat with the opposite ankle.

AFTERWORD

Stay in shape, stay with your program. Although words of encouragement may sometimes seem facile, we believe that the benefits of regular exercise are far greater than the relatively little amount of time and effort needed to maintain physical fitness. After reading and using this book, we hope that you agree with us.

If you are having difficulty maintaining a regular program, some reminders follow:

1. Keep your fitness goals in mind and set realistic ones that will motivate you to exercise regularly.
2. If you miss a scheduled workout, do not feel guilty and discouraged or abandon your program. Simply start exercising again as soon as possible, but reduce the intensity of your workout if more than one week has elapsed between workouts. Build up gradually to your previous level of fitness.
3. Vary your routine. Try different activities until you find a few you enjoy.
4. Exercise with a friend or with friends.

The most important goal is your health and well-being.